MW01322559

Hamburger
Coke

June 8, 2024

Dear Mr. Paley,

As you know, reading is fundamental to all learning. So I encourage you to read as many books as possible this summer. I also hope that you will enjoy the stories in this book. Please forgive all the typos and grammatical errors.

Respectfully,

Ilyong Mom

Hamburger Coke

First Edition First Print October 30, 2021
Author Ilryong Moon (email: skycastlemoon@gmail.com)
Editor Joony Moon
Publisher Gil Su Jang
Distributed in South Korea by Knowledge and Sensibility (지식과감성#)
Publication Registration 2012-000081

Book Cover Illustrations Gyurim Clara Kim
Proofread by Joann V. Kinney, Angela M. Petro
Formatted by Woo Yeon Kim
Designed by Ye Eun Park
Marketed by Eun Bit Ko, Yeon Woo Jung
Address 1212 Daeryung Post Tower 6th, 298 Beokkot-ro, Geumcheon-gu, Seoul, South Korea
Tel 070-4651-3730~4
Fax 070-4325-7006
E-mail ksbookup@naver.com
Homepage www.knsbookup.com

ISBN 979-11-392-0157-4(03810)
Price ₩15,000 in South Korea, $25 in the U.S.A.

Directly to
Homepage of Knowledge and Sensibility

Hamburger Coke

Tales of Poverty and Public Service

One immigrant's journey through Long Hair, Mushu Pork, Height, Soccer Coaching, Elections, and other important lessons along the way

Ilryong Moon
Edited by **Joony Moon**

In Loving Memory of My Mother

| Contents |

Chapter 2

Raising Two Children

Chapter 3

Serving As A School Board Member

Chapter 4

American Education Stories

Chapter 5

Stories Of American Society

Chapter 6

People I Have Met

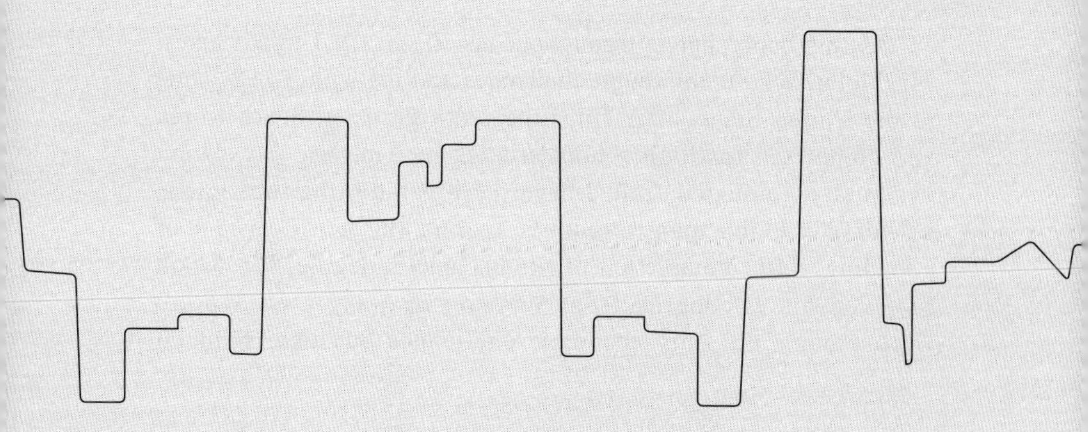

| *Congratulatory Letter* |

Young Jin Cho

Retired Bishop, The United Methodist Church

Congratulations!

As Mr. Moon's former pastor, it is my great honor to write congratulatory remarks on the publication of his book sharing his life story. I have known him for more than thirty years as one of my parishioners, a lawyer, and a faithful public servant.

As this book shares, throughout his life in the United States, Mr. Moon faced many tough challenges and difficulties. He came to the United States after finishing tenth grade in South Korea and completed his high school studies in America. Mr. Moon eventually graduated from Harvard University, the prestigious university which many students around the world dream of attending. After completion of his bachelor's degree, Mr. Moon received his JD degree from William & Mary Law School. He overcame not only academic challenges but also financial difficulties as a first generation immigrant. He truly lived life as a pioneer.

Mr. Moon has his own law practice but is better known as a school board member. He was elected and served five terms for the Fairfax County School Board, which is home to some of the best public schools in America. He effectively served as a school board member and made significant contributions to not only the county's education policies but also to the Korean-American community.

His dream to serve as an elected school board member started by simply attending and observing the school board meetings. I can personally testify to how Mr. Moon faithfully prepared himself to serve and ran the electoral races with courage and vision. As a school board member, he also fought to ensure that students of all cultures and backgrounds within the public school system of Fairfax County were welcomed at school.

This book shares a strong message with the Korean-American community. He challenges us to get out of our comfort zone and to take part in American society. We are here to live as responsible citizens and to contribute to making this great nation greater. Mr. Moon pursued this vision and courageously challenged the barriers he faced. His presence on the school board has been a source of great encouragement to many schoolteachers, and we are proud of him.

In this book we find many names of individuals who helped and encouraged him in his journey to this moment. He has never been a lone ranger. He is indebted to many people to have reached this point. I believe that he intentionally mentions the names of these kind and graceful people to express his deep gratitude to them and to follow in their steps. Mr. Moon also challenges us to become like those individuals to continue to make a difference in others' lives.

Throughout this book, Mr. Moon wants to share his life story and to encourage the next generation. By sharing his experiences, he wants to build up today's youth to be a better and stronger generation. He also wants to provide some information for people in Korea about the education system in the United States. While the Korean version of this book has blessed many people, I hope and pray that the English version of this book will also be a blessing to many people, especially second or third generation Korean-Americans.

Once again, many congratulations on your life and on the publication of this book!

| Recommendation Letter |

Karen K. Garza, PhD
President & CEO of Battelle for Kids
Former Superintendent of Fairfax County Public Schools

I have had the good fortune of working with many extraordinary people. Mr. Ilryong Moon is one of the very special and unique individuals I have been fortunate to know for he has had an indelible impact on my life. In 2013, I was given the opportunity to lead one of the best school districts in the country, Fairfax County Public Schools. Mr. Moon was the Chairman of the School Board, and I am sure that he had a large role in my being provided this opportunity.

I was named the first woman to serve as superintendent of Fairfax County Public Schools. I was always impressed that Mr. Moon would often highlight this fact whenever he would introduce me. He was consistent in his well-placed concern for diversity and inclusion and would often ask for metrics demonstrating our progress for diversifying our leaders in the system.

Mr. Moon is an intelligent, thoughtful, and inclusive leader and person. In his role on the Fairfax County School Board, he was always respectful while also holding system leaders accountable for doing what was right for students—all students. One might think that doing the right thing was always easy, but it wasn't. There were times when doing what was right for students was extraordinarily difficult. As the leader of the school system, I could always count on Mr. Moon to demonstrate courage and stand firm when it really mattered.

I had the unique opportunity to visit Mr. Moon's home country of South Korea with him in the fall of 2014. He wanted to provide me with opportunities to experience the culture and meet with the people of the country he loved. In this book, he tells a story which is true—I did struggle with the food, especially the octopus that was literally moving on the plate when it was served! But the truth is that this trip was an amazing experience. We traveled to all corners of this beautiful country, visited schools, and engaged with many school leaders. It was a once in a lifetime experience!

In this series of essays, you will gain insights into an extraordinary life—that of an immigrant, a father, a son, a professional, and an elected official. I marvel at all that Mr. Moon has accomplished, for his story is the epitome of the "American Dream". He was born in South Korea and grew up there in poverty. He immigrated at the age of seventeen to this country where he became a Harvard-educated attorney and one of the longest serving school board members in Fairfax County Public Schools history.

You will delight in his stories of family and his insights and experiences from many years of public service and contribution.

Enjoy!

| *Preface* |

First, know my intent of publishing this book is not to brag about myself. I also do not pretend to know how to overcome poverty or get into Harvard. Nor am I suggesting what anyone must do to send two sons to Ivy League colleges. I am not claiming that I can provide a roadmap for how a teenage immigrant could eventually serve as an elected official for twenty years in the United States. Everything I share here is my personal story filled with unique struggles and blessings that shaped my own path.

What I can say, however, is that I grew up poor, managed to attend a top college even though I did not immigrate to the U.S. until I was in high school, and am immensely proud of my two sons born in the U.S. Now that I am in my sixties, I feel that I can look back on my life and share with my children, future descendants, and willing readers my experiences as an immigrant, student, parent, and member of the community. I do not claim to know any better than others or hold the perfect answers to solve all of life's challenges and questions, but I hope that the stories that I share in this book will provide something for readers to think about as they face those challenges and questions for themselves.

As such, I would like to tell you a little bit about myself first. I immigrated to the U.S. in the summer of 1974 after finishing my high school sophomore year in Korea. The decision to immigrate stemmed from our family's desire to overcome extreme poverty. My homeland of Korea was poor at that time and —my family even more so. My father's employment situation was dire and unstable.

Once I arrived in the U.S., I had to repeat sophomore year as I learned English and transitioned to an American school. After graduating from high school in 1977, I entered Harvard, from which I was so thankful to have received admission. I started off as a chemistry major but later changed to East Asian Studies as I dreamed about returning to Korea or becoming a diplomat once I completed my studies in the U.S. I was so committed to this goal that I even took a leave of absence to study Chinese in Taiwan. The mainland China was not open to students from the U.S. at that time.

After graduating from Harvard in 1981, I enrolled in law school at William & Mary in Williamsburg, Virginia—the oldest public law school in the country. Ever since graduating from the law school in 1984, I have actively practiced law. I also married and had two sons—one born in 1988 and another in 1991. The older son studied Economics at Harvard, moving on to first work for a management consulting firm before switching careers to work for a non-profit foundation. He then went to UC Berkeley to get a master's degree in public policy. He now lives in the Boston area and works for the Commonwealth of Massachusetts on its SNAP (Supplemental Nutrition Assistance Program), a public policy area he had taken special interest while in graduate school.

My younger son majored in physics at Brown University and then obtained his doctoral degree in physics from the University of Illinois Urbana-Champaign (UIUC) in the spring of 2019. Since graduating, he has worked in the tech industry in Seattle, Washington, and was recruited to work as an applied scientist for one of the largest companies in the world. These days, he works as an artificial intelligence researcher at a small tech startup. Both of my sons graduated from Thomas Jefferson High School for Science and Technology, located in Fairfax County, Virginia, considered to be one of the best high schools in the U.S.

While growing my legal career, I was elected to the Fairfax County School Board in 1995 when Fairfax County first began electing its school board members. The Fairfax County School

Board is the ultimate decision-making body on all operational matters for the public schools in the county. It decides educational policies, adopts the budget, and oversees student and personnel issues. It also hires, directs, supervises, and evaluates the performance of the superintendent. From my research, I believe that I may have been the first Korean American elected to public office on the east coast of the U.S. Though I failed in my bid for reelection four years later, I remained in public service on the Fairfax County Planning Commission, running again for the school board and winning in November 2003.

Since then, I served three more terms on the school board before retiring at the end of 2019. While on the school board, I had the honor of serving as its chairman and vice chairman for three terms each. Counting it all up, I had served for twenty years in a governing role for public education in one of the best school systems in the U.S.

Presiding at School Board meeting as the Chairman

Fairfax County, mentioned in the Korean drama series of Sky Castle, is located near Washington, D.C. As an area that is home to many federal government employees and contractors, as well as other government-related workers, the county boasts some of the highest household income and education levels.[1] Many foreign diplomats reside there, too. As you can imagine, the level of interest in public education and expectation are naturally high in such a place. Some people even liken the Fairfax County school district as the American equivalent of the 'Gangnam 8th School District' in Korea.

In terms of the number of students, it ranks tenth out of about fifteen thousand school districts in the U.S. It educates over one hundred eighty thousand students with an annual budget of almost $3.6 billion and employs over twenty-five thousand people. The county's population is racially and culturally diverse, with students coming from 204 countries and speaking over two hundred different languages. It is like the United Nations. The Fairfax County students are lucky to study in such a wonderful learning environment for future global leaders.

Now backed with a summary glimpse of my story, the book that follows here is filled with stories that will give you access to specific moments in my life that really bring color to it all. I have been regularly writing columns in Korean in The Korea Times-Washington, D.C. since August 2010. Through those columns, I have wanted to share my experience, and the information I have been able to access in my position as a school board member. Of course, I missed my submission deadlines a few times, especially when traveling out of town, and on a few other occasions, I resubmitted previously published ones. Prior to 2010, I also contributed columns to a local Korean community weekly paper

1 Per the 2020 data, the county population is about 1.17 million. Sixty-one percent of the residents twenty-five years or older have college degrees, with about a half of them having advanced degrees. The median annual household income exceeds one hundred twenty thousand dollars.

and AM1310, a local Korean radio station.

All along, I knew that I was not a professional writer, and my columns might not have always been of superb quality. However, my desire to be helpful to other Koreans in the Washington, D.C. area on education issues helped me overcome any potential embarrassment. I still write for The Korea Times-Washington, D.C. today, and my columns have sometimes been re-published on other locally affiliated Korea Times across the U.S.

I am only able to share a small part of the more than seven hundred columns written over that span. I hope that the stories appearing in this book will be helpful to the other Korean Americans living not only in Fairfax County, but in other parts of the U.S. and the parents and students in Korea as well.

Some information and statistics cited in the book may be outdated by the time you read it. Therefore, I have provided footnotes where applicable. However, the purpose of publishing this book is not to provide such information or statistical data, but to share a snapshot of the thoughts I had at the time I was writing the columns. I have therefore purposely avoided rewriting the columns from the present view. I have also included several new stories in this book to provide additional helpful points and context—these are the ones that appear without any original publication dates.

I want to take a moment to express my appreciation to: The Korea Times, AM1310, and Washington Media, which have provided me the platforms and outlets to publish my columns. Writing columns has provided me with incredible, priceless opportunities to think through my thoughts and be of public service to the local Korean American community. I would like to thank all those readers who loyally read and listened to my columns over the years. Their constant encouragement and advice have been sources of energy for me to continue serving the community for more than two decades.

I also want to note my deep gratitude to the now-retired Bishop Young Jin Cho of the Virginia Annual Conference of United

Methodist Church, and Dr. Karen Garza, Former Superintendent of the Fairfax County Public Schools and CEO of Battelle for Kids. They have provided me with their congratulatory and recommendation letters in support of this book. I want to thank Anne Holton, Professor of Education Policy and former Interim President of George Mason University and former Virginia Secretary of Education; Patrick Welsh, a writer and my former English teacher from T.C. Williams Senior High School; Ryan McElveen, a former colleague of mine on the Fairfax County School Board; and Tom Gjelten, a writer and a retired journalist from NPR, for graciously providing me with their endorsements for the book.

Furthermore, I want to note my gratitude for the advice and support provided by Mr. Moon Kyu Shin, former Education Minister at the Korean Embassy here in the Washington, D.C.; Mr. Kap Yong Cho, former President of Busan Center for Promotion of Gifted and Talented Education; Ms. Ui Jung Chung, Director of Policy, Incheon Metropolitan City Office of Education; Ms. Hyekyung Huh, an education consultant in the U.S.; Ms. Mi Hyun Kim and Mr. Jinwook Choi, education consultants both in Korea; Ms. Sun Joo Lee, a retired ESL teacher in New Jersey; Mr. Tae Wook Park, President of The Korea Times-Washington, D.C.; and Mr. Tae Hyun Kim, a parent in Fairfax County passionate about education. A special recognition goes to Gyurim Clara Kim for the drawing on the front cover and Ms. So Jeong Jeong for her help on the design for the book cover.

Of course, this translated version of the original book in Korean published in October of 2020 would not have been possible without the help from Ms. Wanda Park, a classmate of mine from the middle school in Korea who now resides in Toronto, Canada, for the initial translation, Joonyoung Moon, my newlywed first son for his tremendous work of editing, and Joann Kinney and Angela Petro for proofreading. Joann and Angela directly supported me in the school board office while I was a school board member, and they are the best proofreaders with whom I have ever worked.

Lastly, a special thanks goes to an old friend of mine, Kwang Yul Choi, the CEO of ENC, Inc. in California, for generously providing me with the free shipping of both the Korean and the English versions of the books from Korea.

Chapter 1

Immigrating To The U.S. And Studying

The only time that I saw my father cry was after my second younger brother died. It was in 1967 when I was in the fourth grade. My father does not express his emotions well—he did not even cry when his wife, my mother, passed away. It is perhaps because he had lived a difficult and lonely life for a long time. He had originally lived in North Korea with his widowed mother and two brothers. When the Korean War broke out, he headed south all by himself. He was seventeen years old at the time.

But his reaction was different when my second younger brother died at the age of four from encephalitis.[2] My father hopelessly watched his youngest child die, as we were too poor to seek medical help. Our family of five lived at the time in a single rented room in a shanty area in Munrae-dong, Youngdeungpo-gu, Seoul. My father was unemployed, and my mother used to sell wool yarn out of a basket, earning the only income on which our family relied.

The whole neighborhood was dirty, smelly, and unsanitary, with black sewage from a nearby factory running across the

2 Encephalitis is inflammation of the active tissues of the brain caused by an infection or an autoimmune response. The inflammation causes the brain to swell, which can lead to headache, stiff neck, sensitivity to light, mental confusion and seizures. Encephalitis can be caused by infections or autoimmune conditions where the body's own immune responses attack the brain. Even with extensive testing, the specific cause of encephalitis remains unknown in about 30%-40% of cases. Encephalitis can also result from certain viruses carried by mosquitoes, ticks and other insects or animals.
(https://www.hopkinsmedicine.org/health/conditions-and-diseases/encephalitis)
It used to be a deadly disease in Korea for many years, especially for young children living in poor, unsanitary areas.

neighborhood. My younger brother was cremated, as we were not in a financial position to purchase a burial spot for him. My father scattered his ashes in the Han River. My parents had lost two sons within five years. My first younger brother died due to meningitis before his first birthday. I was seven years old at the time. So, I have lost two younger brothers as well.[3]

I do not have much memory about my first younger brother as I was too young at the time of his death, but I am so heartbroken whenever I think about my second younger brother. Around the time my second younger brother was living, Korea was experiencing a food shortage and was relying on food aid from the U.S. One of the pieces of aid we received was corn bread given to students at school. We did not have any snacks at home, and we could barely afford to eat three meals a day—it was luxury to even think about snacks like cookies, bread, or fruit. The corn bread, the only snack we got once a week, was quite tasty. I used to split the corn bread with my little brother.

My young brother somehow remarkably remembered the distribution dates of the corn bread and eagerly waited for me to return home with his share. The distance between my school and home was quite far. I would eat the bread little by little while walking home. I thought to myself that I was entitled to half of the bread, but I would finish my share long before reaching home and became so tempted to eat a little bit more. "Well, I am bigger than he, so I have the right to eat more," I would justify to myself and take another bite and then more bites off corners. As I did not like the shape of bread left after such bites, I would take

3 I have two younger sisters, with one born before, and another born after, the two brothers I lost.

even more bites to make it a square. The bread would eventually become a tiny piece by the time I arrived at home. Without knowing what had transpired, my brother would still gratefully take that tiny piece of bread left. It is so sad that he died without receiving any medical treatment. Only after my brother's death did the local government health department officials finally come out to quarantine and disinfect the area.

After my second younger brother's death, my father went to work in Vietnam during the Vietnam War as a civilian technician. Our living condition improved while he worked in Vietnam, allowing us to purchase our first house near the Guro Industrial Park.[4] However, he was again unable to secure a stable job after returning home, and we ended up having to sell the house. My father decided to immigrate to the U.S. when the proceeds from the sale of the house almost ran out. My mother even sold her jewelry to pay for my school tuition when I was in the eighth grade. The last place I lived in Korea before coming to the U.S. was a housing complex where a group of six to seven families lived together under the same roof, with each family having one room and a kitchen. More than twenty people shared one water tap and one outhouse. Of course, there was no hot water, no shower, and no bathtub.

To overcome poverty, we left Korea and immigrated to the U.S.

4 Guro Industrial Park is in the southern part of Seoul, Korea. When it was first built there, the area was known as one of the poorest parts of Seoul.

A group picture of the youth group of the church in my neighborhood taken after a service in 1973, about a year before I came to the U.S. I am on the far right.

The Day Of Immigration

AM 1310
July 2000

It has been twenty-six years since I immigrated to the U.S. After completing tenth grade, we boarded a Northwest Airlines flight from Seoul to the U.S. Around midnight on Aug. 30, 1974, I, along with my mother and two younger sisters, finally arrived at Dulles Airport in northern Virginia. "Wow! This is the U.S.A.!" I was amazed at seeing so many cars neatly parked in the airport parking lot. My father, who had obtained the work visa and come to the U.S. a year earlier, was waiting at the airport to pick us up with his own car—a white Plymouth that seemed like a bus.

Not only did we never own a car in Korea, but even a cab ride had been a rare occasion for our family. You can imagine my astonishment seeing that we now owned a car. I was fascinated with the different gauges on the dashboard. I noticed that my father would add two quarts of engine oil into the car every week. I first thought that all cars required new engine oil each week but soon learned that it was because the car was old. My father only paid a few hundred dollars for the used car, and he did not know much about cars to begin with.

This is how my immigrant life began twenty-six years ago. Our rented apartment did not have any furniture in it. When we left Korea, we only had twenty dollars, and that was all the money we had left after selling all our belongings. I was responsible for taking care of the money because I was the eldest son. I needed to take a cab on the last day in Korea. I forgot to bring to Gimpo Airport[5] the chest x-rays[6] we were required to provide for entry into the U.S. at the time, and therefore had to rush back to my cousin's house to pick them up. However, I did not have enough money for the cab fare. Had my cousin not lent me the money, we would have missed the flight.

Looking back at the humble beginning of our life in the U.S., I now have so many things to be thankful for. I am thankful to the U.S. for providing me with the opportunity for a better life. Of course, what I can enjoy now is a result of the hard work and sacrifices made by my parents. My mother cleaned hotel rooms, school buildings, and even private homes, simultaneously working more than two full-time jobs for many years. My father tried to save lunch money by eating bologna sandwiches he brought from home for twenty-five years until his retirement. I am grateful that the U.S. had given me and my sisters the chance to attend college. The U.S. provides a fair chance to everyone regardless of racial background. That is how I could become the first Asian American elected official in Fairfax County, Virginia, without needing to pull any strings. Of course, there are still many areas needing improvement but the payout is fair if you work hard.

---

5 This was long before the Incheon International Airport was built.

6 Chest x-rays were required for Koreans to immigrate to the U.S. at that time because of prevalence of tuberculosis in Korea.

With my father at a Korean restaurant in Fairfax County (2013)

My Mother

The Korea Times-Washington, D.C.
May 4, 2012

I attended the meeting sponsored by the Custodial Services Advisory Council last week. This group acts as an advisory body to the Fairfax County School Board. The council often discusses cleaning services and facility management and makes recommendations to the School Board. As the new chairman of the budget committee of the School Board, I wanted to share the budget development discussion for the following year and hear feedback from the attendees at the council's meeting.

I noticed two men who looked Korean amongst the roughly forty people in attendance. Their greetings of me with smiles made me feel more comfortable. As I had rarely seen Koreans at this type of meetings, I was grateful for their presence. After the meeting, one of them came up to me. He handed me a note after a brief introduction, and I became emotional upon reading the note.

The note seemed to have been written during the meeting, but the sentence structure and the grammar were nearly perfect, and the points conveyed in the note were very logical. I could feel the sorrow of immigrants in that short note. We often say that all honest jobs are equally honorable, but I immediately felt in that moment that this man would not have been working as a school custodian if he had still been living in Korea. The reality of immigrant life must have forced him to take on whatever job he could find. Knowing that there are many people like him within the Fairfax County Public Schools, my heart was crushed.

Last week was the first anniversary of my mother's passing. My mother had worked as a cleaner for a long time since arriving in the U.S. Growing up in rural Korea, she did not have opportunities for much formal education, like many other women during that era in Korea. As such, there was not much of a selection of jobs available for her, but she worked hard as a cleaner. We settled down in Alexandria, Virginia. My mother woke up early in the morning to prepare breakfast and pack lunch for everyone in the family. She even prepared dinner before heading out to go to work at a hotel in Crystal City. My mother had to ride a bus to work as the only car that we owned was used by my father for going to his work in Washington, D.C.

My mother worked eight hours cleaning rooms and bathrooms at the hotel, but she did not come home right away when her shift ended. She took a bus to Landmark Shopping Center, passing back across where we lived on the way. She would then transfer to another bus and eventually get off at the bus stop across from the Northern Virginia Community College in Annandale. She would walk up the hill for three quarters of a mile to a private school where the Jewish Community Center is currently located. It was a small school, but the work was hard as she was the sole cleaner. I am sure that she would be exhausted by the time she arrived there as she had already had a long day.

After my father came home from his work, we often went to the school to help her. However, my mother never let me clean the restroom. Perhaps she did not trust that I could do the job well, but, most likely, she did not want her son to clean the restroom. She used to say that cleaning jobs should end in her generation.

Mother's cleaning job did not end at the hotel or the school. While others enjoyed the time off on weekends, she worked as a housekeeper for private homes. She wanted to do all she could to support the family on household expenses and to save money for her three children's college education. But she had to quit her job as a housekeeper one day, after she mistakenly misused the cleaning chemicals and damaged the carpet in one of the houses that she cleaned.[7] Her anxious words about possibly having to pay for the damages remain in my heart.

May 5th is Children's Day in Korea. The following Sunday

is Mother's Day in the U.S. There will be no mothers without children; but then again, you cannot think of a child without a mother. So, I think about my mother even on Children's Day. There is nothing greater than the love and the sacrifice of a mother. As we celebrate Children's Day and Mother's Day, let us always remember our mothers and reflect on our lives whether we are doing our jobs well enough as parents ourselves.

I miss my mother even more in May.

On my mother's birthday

7 Many years after this incident, at one of my campaign events, I met the couple of the house that my mother used to clean. The husband was a well-known politician in the local area. He also was one of the first individuals to whom I paid a visit when running for the first election. Of course, I chose not to tell them about my mother's story, and they did not seem to remember her anyway.

Nurungji (Scorched Rice)

The Korea Times–Washington, D.C.
November 9, 2018

I recently visited Korea for about ten days. For several years, I have visited Korea annually with key educators from Fairfax County Public Schools to introduce Korea to them. This year I was accompanied by the superintendent and one of the regional assistant superintendents. It was their first visit to Korea. Our tour started with Seoul, Incheon, and the Gyeonggi Province areas and included Sejong, Yeosu, Naju, Gyeongju, Busan, Gimhae, Geoje, Chuncheon, and Wonju. We travelled all over Korea under a tight schedule.

The superintendent was hired by the School Board around a year and half ago. He preferred not to be away from his office for too long during his first year in Fairfax County and therefore wanted to wait until this year for the travel to Korea. There are five regional assistant superintendents in Fairfax County Public Schools with each assistant superintendent in charge of roughly forty schools. The regional assistant superintendent who visited Korea this year has the Langley, Marshall, Oakton, Madison, and South Lake High Schools pyramids under his supervision.

The main reason I regularly take senior educators of the school system to Korea is that I see the need for them to learn about Korea. There are not many school districts in the U.S. as racially and culturally diverse as Fairfax County Public Schools. Asian students comprise about twenty percent of the total student population today and the percentage is predicted to continue to increase. Korean students make up about four to five percent. The importance of multicultural education for the senior educators cannot, therefore, be emphasized enough.

During our visits to Korea, we observe classes and meet with Korean educators to exchange our respective views on education issues of mutual interest. Our Fairfax County educators get to experience not only the fast-moving life of urban areas in Korea but also the beautiful autumn scenery of rural parts of the country as well as various Korean foods and the warm hospitality exhibited by Korean people. As they learn more about Korea during the trip, they get to better understand and have more empathy toward Korean students and their parents within Fairfax County. That is why I gladly volunteer to guide their trips and put in the effort to introduce my home country to them.

There is no fund allocated by the school system to support these trips, so I need to find sponsors. In return for such sponsorships, we deliver lectures, hold seminars, and make presentations in various schools, colleges, and educational research institutes. Some of the expenses are even covered by personal friends of mine. For this year's trip, the two education officials at the Korean Embassy in Washington, D.C. also went out of their way to help make the trip possible. I would like to thank everyone, including those two Korean Embassy officials, who supported us.

I also would like to share something experienced by our educators this year during a luncheon hosted by the Deputy Superintendent of the metropolitan city of Daegu. The last dish served was "stone pot rice." The rice is cooked with sweet potatoes with ginkgo nuts mixed in it. Once the rice has been removed from the stone pot, you pour hot water on the top of the nurungji (scorched rice) still left at the bottom of the pot. You then wait for a while so that the rice becomes soft after being soaked with the hot water. Koreans call that softened rice nurungbap. Obviously, the two Fairfax County educators had never seen nurungji or nurungbap before and were fascinated by the whole process and how good it tasted.

I explained to them a bit more about nurungji. Nurungji and nurungbap are enjoyed by many Koreans. I told them that I used to eat nurungji as a snack, sometimes sprinkling some sugar on it to add flavor. We would intentionally burn the rice to make nurungji. On the other hand, nurungji was also a symbol of poverty. Nurungji is on most occasions considered to be the leftover rice that is stuck to the bottom of the pot. You would only eat it because there was no other food available. We have a saying that goes "I don't even have any nurungji to eat." to describe a situation of lacking food or a level of poverty.

Korea has not always been economically well off. There were times when people worried about their next meals, and my own family was no exception. My mother often waited for everybody else in the family to finish their meals first and then filled her hungry stomach with nurungji. She would pour in more water to nurungji when there was not much nurungji left—she was filling her stomach with water. Nurungji possessed dual meanings.

I could sense from their body language that the superintendent and the assistant superintendent must have felt something in their heart after listening to my explanation. Poverty did not only exist a long time ago in Korea. You can see it every day in many parts of the world. We also need to keep in mind that it exists even in Fairfax County, considered to be one of the wealthiest counties in the U.S.

My Second Grade Teacher

AM 1310
August 31, 2000

I took a two-week vacation and visited Korea earlier this month. My last visit to Korea was to celebrate my father-in-law's seventieth birthday in 1993—it has been seven years since then. My wife and two sons had been in Korea for a few weeks before I joined them. I had already witnessed the rapid changes in Korea during my prior visits, so there was no surprise this time around.

This year's visit was beneficial to my sons as they were now old enough to enjoy their parents' home country and make their own memories. They were too young to do so seven years ago. But most of all, this trip was meant to spend time with my father-in-law before too late as his health was declining.

In addition to celebrating my father-in-law's birthday, there was another meaningful plan with this visit—I wanted to meet up with my second-grade teacher. She was around my mother's age and was always very generous with me. There was a debt that I still owed her, and I wanted to repay it. However, I did not have any information about her other than her name.

For many months leading up to my trip to Korea, I had tried to locate her by reaching out to education officials at the Korean Embassy in Washington, D.C. without any luck. She had left her teaching job a long time ago, and even her last known address was unclear. However, when I approached a Korean prosecutor who was my acquaintance and explained the situation, he was thankfully able to locate my teacher.

I was finally able to meet my teacher for lunch at a restaurant near where she was living outside the capital city of Seoul. She did not seem to have changed much from the last time I had seen her more than thirty years ago. I thought that she would show signs of her age, but she looked healthy, bright, and certainly much younger than her age.

When I was in the second grade, I used to love telling old stories. She recognized my talent in storytelling and would set aside some time each day for me to tell stories to my classmates so that I could continue developing presentation skills. Her encouragement may have helped mold me into becoming a lawyer and not being afraid of speaking in front of people. She also bought me a set of books made with thick and good-quality paper. The three-volume set consisted of Origin of Mankind, Universe, and The Animal Kingdom. Knowing that I came from a poor family, she told me that there was no rush to pay her back.

Not having paid for the books for all these years, I finally wanted to pay her back. Upon seeing her, I handed her an envelope with payment in it. I shared with her how I longed to see her again and to pay her back for the books, but she refused to accept the envelope. She said that she had no recollection of my debt and then thanked me for remembering her after all these years, claiming that she was just an ordinary teacher with many human faults.

She even confided in me of her fear now that, if a student like I remembered something that she had no recollection of, there would certainly be many students, to whom she clearly remembered having said and done things that she should not have, would remember her for all the hurtful things she had done—and that was terrifying her.

Oh, wow! The words of my second-grade teacher on that day taught me another valuable lesson and made me reflect deeply on my own life.

Mr. Patrick Welsh And Learning English

The Korea Times-Washington, D.C.
February 24, 2011

I attended a panel discussion sponsored by the U.S. Civil Rights Commission a few weeks ago. One of the main topics was racism and impact of school disciplines on minority students. The teachers, principals, and education administrators selected from various parts of the country participated in the presentations.

The classroom teachers went first and the last presenting teacher looked familiar to me, even from behind. I quickly glanced through the program and noticed that the final speaker was Mr. Patrick Welsh, my English teacher from T.C. Williams Senior High School[8] in Alexandria, Virginia. He was now all gray-haired but was still at the same school where he had been for the past forty years. He had always been so kind to me.[9] He had a law degree but chose to devote his life to teaching instead of practicing law.

I immigrated to the U.S. in 1974 in the middle of high school. Learning English was not easy, and I experienced difficulties with pronunciations, especially with the "r" sound as the Korean language does not have that sound. I could not roll up my tongue no matter how hard I tried. One day, Mr. Welsh took me into the principal's office and, out of blue, asked the principal to say, "park a car". The principal, Mr. Robert Hanley, a native of the New England area in the northeastern part of the U.S., said it without any 'r' sound. Mr. Welsh quickly turned to me and said, "Well, you

---

8 The name of the school was changed to Alexandria City High School as of July 1, 2021.

9 Mr. Patrick Welsh retired in 2013 after teaching for forty-five years.

see, you are not the only one having difficulty in pronouncing an 'r'. Mr. Hanley was born in the U.S. and yet cannot do it, either." Mr. Welsh's words were a huge encouragement.

Mr. Patrick Welsh, my English teacher
at T.C. Williams Senior High School (1977)

Mr. Welsh regularly gave his students vocabulary lists to memorize for homework. As I felt an urgency to learn English more quickly, I requested additional lists of words that I should learn. I knew that I was far behind my native-born classmates and needed to work harder to catch up with them. Mr. Welsh never hesitated to honor my requests. Not only had he prepared extra lists, but he had also personally recorded the pronunciations of all the words on the lists on cassette tapes for me. His help and encouragement became an additional motivation for me to study even harder. Reminiscing about those old days studying with Mr. Welsh, who now often writes education columns in the newspapers such as Washington Post and USA Today, I cannot help but feel that time has flown by so fast as my own two sons are now even older than I was when I first met him.

English is the most important subject. Without English, you cannot demonstrate your capability in other subjects. No matter how good you are in math or science, it will be useless if you cannot comprehend the words and sentences around them or explain the concepts in English. Therefore, I emphasize to everyone that they should try to learn English as thoroughly and quickly as possible.

Students new to the U.S. must make an extra effort. They need to read a lot and look up the words that they do not know in the dictionary right away, and they should try to use their newly learned words as much as possible. Those words will not remain in the memory too long if not practiced. I also would like to encourage all students to maintain good relationships with their teachers regardless of the subject. Demonstrate to your teachers how hard you are trying to learn and do not be afraid to ask for help whenever needed. No teacher would reject the earnest requests for help from hard-working students.

The importance of learning English is not solely for students, though. It is for all immigrants regardless of their ages. Competency in English is necessary to compete with native-born Americans. There still are many words that I do not know even though I have studied English since high school and have lived in the U.S. for thirty-seven years. I have put dictionaries in several places around my house. I try to look up any new or unclear word in the dictionary right away. Of course, native-born Americans do not know every word, either, and we cannot learn every word no matter how hard we try—but immigrants can never catch up with the natives without putting in the extra effort.

Giving special recognition to Mr. Patrick Welsh at an orientation for new Fairfax County teachers (2014)

Mr. Louis Kokonis

The Korea Times-Washington, D.C.
March 11, 2016

Two weeks ago, I visited T.C. Williams High School (T.C.) in Alexandria, Virginia. It is the same school that was featured in the famous movie *Remember the Titans*. I am a graduate of the school and wanted to go see one of my old teachers that day. I noticed numerous changes made to the school. A new building had been erected beside the old one about ten years ago at the cost of ninety million dollars. All classrooms and facilities are now located in this new building while the old building had been demolished and turned into a parking garage.

Mr. Louis Kokonis showing how to solve a problem

Mr. Kokonis was teaching calculus when I walked into his classroom. He had taught a pre-calculus course called Algebra 5 during my junior year there. He is now eighty-four years old and in his fifty-seventh year of teaching. He has taught at T.C. for forty-eight years and at another school for nine years prior to coming to T.C. He told me that he just loved teaching and would like to continue to do it for at least one more year.[10]

There will be a one-week AP[11] Physics class offered to teachers in the upcoming summer break, and Mr. Kokonis is planning to take it. He heard that calculus and differential equations were used a lot in AP Physics and would like to check it out personally. He also shared that he was spending a lot of time preparing for his differential equations class. I assumed that, with his almost sixty years of teaching, he would not need much preparation at all, but he was still putting in a lot of time to prepare, making me feel a greater level of respect for his professionalism.

I could recall Mr. Kokonis from forty years ago, always being covered with white chalk powder. He used to clear the chalkboard with his hands rather than using an eraser. He would then wipe off his hands on his pants, hence the chalk powder on his whole body. There was one incident from back then where I was engaged in a fight with a white classmate. He was much taller and bigger than me and used to tease me by calling me "a stupid Korean," telling me to go back to Korea. He thought that he was just having fun. One day after the class, however, I could no longer tolerate his behavior, so I grabbed his neck and pushed him hard against the wall. Mr. Kokonis witnessed the whole incident and intervened to stop the fight. Thankfully, he did not discipline me, though.

---

10 In January 2019, I attended a reception in honor of his sixtieth anniversary of teaching. A fund was raised to give out the scholarships in his name. As of October 2021, he is still teaching and eighty nine years old.

11 AP refers to Advanced Placement and is a term applied to courses considered to be at college level.

I sat down in the back and observed his class for an hour. He was no longer using white chalk, so his pants were clean. His students looked serious and were giving him full attention. There were seventeen students in the class, with an even number of male and female students. It seemed that there had been an increase in the number of female students in higher-level math classes compared to when I was there.

T.C. is the only public high school in Alexandria and white students make up only about twenty percent of the student body. I noticed in the Mr. Kokonis's class that around half of the students were white, with the remaining students split between Asians and Middle Easterners. There was one black student. Bearing in mind that the black students made up about thirty-five percent of the school, there still was an achievement gap in math for black students.

Thinking about the old days, Mr. Kokonis shared with me that the students from Korea and Vietnam who started to arrive to the U.S. in the mid-1970s had been particularly good in math. These days, students from the Middle East and India were good in math, too, he said. T.C. still has a high percentage of underprivileged black and Hispanic students as was the case forty years ago.

Worried about the level of academic achievement, some middle-class families are reluctant to send their children to T.C.; yet the hard-working students from T.C. still get accepted to the top colleges. In my graduating year, two students were admitted to Harvard. Our class also included students who went to Princeton, MIT, Brown, and UPenn. These college acceptance results were as good as any high school in Fairfax County at the time.

It was such a pleasure to see again the old teacher who had always shown kindness to me when I was having a tough time adjusting to immigrant life. His never-changing passion for teaching even in his eighties became a new motivation for me. I guess I should remain active and not retire until I'm ninety.

With Mr. Louis Kokonis at the orientation for new
Fairfax County teachers where I spoke (2019)

Long Hair

The Korea Times-Washington, D.C.
July 7, 2011

I would like to share a picture. It is one of the pictures that I treasure the most. It is a Polaroid picture, but I do not recollect why this was taken. In any case, it was taken on the bleachers of the football field of T.C. Williams High School, Alexandria. It dates to the spring of 1976 when I was a junior there, so about twenty months after I had immigrated to the U.S.

As you can see in the picture, my hair was quite long at the time. Some might think that I took the last train of the hippie era, but that was not the case. When I first arrived in the U.S., my hair was not as short as the other students in Korea but certainly not that long, either. A peculiar circumstance caused me to let my hair grow so long.

There were not any Korean-operated barbershops near my home when I first came to the U.S. in 1974. So, I would have had to go to an American-run barbershop. However, I did not have the confidence in my English skills to describe what style I wanted. I was somewhat obsessed with inferiority and did not want to be embarrassed. It sounds ridiculous when I think about it now. Anyway, I kept postponing the haircut. Even though a Korean-owned barbershop opened for business the following year, I had gotten used to the long hair, and it no longer bothered me —so I let my hair grow longer.

During the three years of high school in the U.S., I did not suffer with an inferiority complex in school despite my poor language skills. Native speaker classmates respected me as I excelled in math and science, even receiving many awards.

However, the situation changed considerably after I entered college. Unlike in high school, it seemed that all students at Harvard were academically excellent in every subject, not just in English. I would not dare to raise my hand and ask questions in class mainly due to my complex about English. I found most of my writing assignments incredibly stressful. They were often returned to me with red marks everywhere. At times, I just felt like quitting school. I avoided interactions with classmates because I was so conscious about my heavy Korean accent, sloppy pronunciation, and grammatical mistakes. I often ended up going to nearby MIT and spending more time with the Korean friends there.

My challenges with English continued into law school. Most of my classes at the law school were taught through the Socratic method, where professors would call on students to stand up and endure long and tortuous question and answer sessions. They felt like interrogations. You could feel cold sweat running down from your head to your toes, and your whole lower body would be paralyzed. Now, I can laugh and joke about it, but at the time, each day and class were a battle— I truly dreaded to go to those classes.

There are a lot of people struggling to overcome difficulties with English. It is even more so for those who come to the U.S.

at an older age. It is not hard to find people even with outgoing personalities avoiding other people and isolating themselves because of their language abilities. Personalities get affected, and passive behaviors often surface. Those struggling with language difficulties need our closer attention and warm encouragement.

My unintentional long hair style met an abrupt end in the spring of 1976. The science department chairman of the school encouraged me to apply for the Governor's School during the summer break. I was going to be the only student recommended from my school for the math and science program.[12] I needed to attach a headshot on the application form, and I did not have the courage to use one with long hair. After much thought, I finally decided to have a haircut. That was how my days of long hair ended, leaving this single picture as memorabilia of those times.

12 The Governor's School program in Virginia started in 1973. In 1976 when I participated, there were only three locations. Now, it is offered at forty locations.

Self-Advocacy

The Korea Times-Washington, D.C.
July 6, 2018

We had an oath ceremony for newly elected members of the Fairfax City Council and the Fairfax City School Board last Friday evening. I attended this event as a liaison from the Fairfax County School Board to the Fairfax City School Board. However, I also wanted to personally congratulate the two newly elected Korean city council members.

Fairfax City is a small city with a population of about twenty-five thousand. It has its own school board, but the Fairfax County School Board is responsible for the actual provision of public education to the students living in the city. Under an agreement between the city and county, the Fairfax City School Board pays the tuition and other charges to the Fairfax County School Board for the city's students.

The importance of the city, geographically located right in middle of the county, cannot be underestimated. In fact, the major administrative offices of the Fairfax County government, central office of the Fairfax County school system, and the courthouse were all previously located within the current boundary of the city. In other words, the city was the most prominent place within the county until its status was elevated to become an independent city from a township in 1961. Now, with two out of the six members of the council being Koreans, the Korean community in the city is enjoying increased recognition. I am hoping for more Korean Americans to run for office and to be elected in the future.[13]

---

13 The term for these two Korean councilmen was two years. They both were re-elected in June 2020.

Self-advocacy is absolutely a needed tool to run for office. The voters judge and vote for candidates based upon the candidates' campaign platforms, personal and public achievements, and other qualifications, which can all go unnoticed without aggressive self-advocacy. Therefore, as we educate our children, we may need to re-examine how our children handle self-advocacy.

I immigrated to the U.S. in the middle of my high school years. I found it quite difficult to adapt to the new environment for a long time. One of the difficulties I faced was changing my attitude toward self-advocacy. I am still awkward talking about my achievements even after almost twenty years of serving as an elected official and living in the U.S. for forty-four years. Humility is a virtue that I was taught and grew up with while in Korea. Bragging about myself to others is always uncomfortable for me.

The following episode occurred when I was in high school here in the U.S. I was elected at the end of my junior year to be the vice president of our school's National Honor Society[14] because my classmates remembered me as a smart student and voted for me. I served in that position for one year during my senior year. Toward the end of my senior year, we had to elect a new president and vice president. The faculty advisor asked the current president and vice president to explain their respective roles and share some of the accomplishments each was able to achieve to give an idea to the potential candidates as to what the positions entailed.

After the president gave her speech, it was my turn. I did not know what to say, though. I started by saying that "the most important duty of the vice president was to assist the president." I then continued my remarks with, "I was not sure whether I had done my job well during my term, but, most likely, my performance was lackluster in many ways, and I must apologize for it." That might have been a perfect, textbook-like speech in Korean culture where humility was emphasized, but the faculty advisor quickly interrupted me right then before I could finish

14 Only the students with good grades can join the National Honor Society.

my remarks. He then continued to explain further about the role of the vice president. He must have thought that my approach was inappropriate for the occasion.

This cultural difference was also apparent in my college classes and seminars. I hesitated to raise my hand and answer questions from the teaching assistants when I felt that the questions were too simple. On the other hand, American students eagerly answered even the minor questions with confidence and provided lengthy explanations. I often wondered about whether there were any education benefits from asking and answering questions on obvious things. American children are taught from an early age not to be afraid to voice their opinions, a huge cultural difference from how I had grown up.

Korean students raised and educated in the U.S. might think differently than the ones brought up in Korea, but they could still be influenced by their parents holding onto their traditional Korean cultural value and approaches. I am not saying that being humble is a terrible thing. Humility is a virtue that must be taught. Yet self-advocacy is an absolute requirement in a highly competitive society and needs to be well taught. Our children will need it whether they are looking for a job, applying for a scholarship, or even running for office. There are times when you must prove that you are better than your competitors. We always need to be sincere with our words, but the traditional Korean view that "fewer words spoken are weightier" is not always true.

A Guy Who Only Hung Around With American Friends

AM 1310
August 13, 2000

I attended George Washington Junior High School during my first year in the U.S. as a sophomore. There were only two Korean students at the school, a girl and me. We did not really have a chance to get to know each other as there was an age gap between us. When I moved up to T.C. Williams Senior High School ("T.C.") for my junior year, I was able to find many more Korean students there.

Most of the Korean students at T.C. were similarly new to the country, so we had a good relationship with each other easily and spent a lot of time together. We had lunch together in the cafeteria and visited each other's houses after school. We played sports on weekends as well. We even formed a social club that met regularly so that we could spend time together. Come to think about it, we met almost every weekend.

However, there was one Korean student there who did not hang around with the fellow Koreans. He was of my age and came to the U.S. at around the same time I did. As he did not spend time with us at all, we used to talk about him behind his back. "He acts as if he knows it all!" "Does he think that he can become American if he only hangs out with Americans?" "That's why someone like him is called a banana, yellow outside but white inside." We used to badmouth him even though we had never met him in person or asked him about the reasons for his behavior.

I used to think that he was being foolish, but come to think of it, he was being smart. He must have realized from early on that hanging out with other Korean-speaking students would not benefit him in learning English. Sure, it would be fun to hang out with friends speaking the same languagc. However, learning English as quickly as possible should have been our top priority to prepare for college. I spoke Korean whenever I hung out with other Korean students and that was taking a considerable amount of time away from the more urgent need to learn and practice English.

I frequently observe Korean students only spending time together with other Koreans even in these days. I am not saying that hanging out with other Koreans is bad. However, you need to think twice about it if you are doing it without also learning English. If you came to live in the U.S., you must focus on learning English first. Of course, we should not forget our roots, and it is also not necessary to ban ourselves from having a good relationship with other fellow Koreans. Moreover, making new friends with native-born Americans may not be always easy when you are not comfortable with communicating in English. That is why we need to be brave and take courageous steps to improve our language skills. Exercising courage must not be delayed.

Part Time Job While In High School

The Korea Times-Washington, D.C.
July 27, 2018

I held part-time jobs while in high school forty-some years ago. My first job was in the first year after immigrating to the U.S. as a housekeeper at a hospital. I learned how to use various cleaning equipment at that time. While cleaning the blood-covered floor of the emergency room, I witnessed seriously ill patients and the doctors running to treat them. I used to sing to control my rising fear every time I had to clean the corridor near the morgue.

My second part-time job was as a cashier at a large variety store during my high school senior year. I needed to save some money because a friend and I planned to visit Korea after graduation. My friend, who was much bigger than I, worked at the front counter and I, at the pharmacy in the back where the customer traffic was relatively less. One of the duties at the pharmacy was selling money orders.[15] I was supposed to issue money orders in the exact same amounts that the customers paid for in cash.

One day, I made a mistake of writing an incorrect amount on the money order and had to prepare a new one—but in doing so, I made another mistake by tearing up and throwing away the voided money order in the garbage can instead of keeping it for our records. The store manager came to me near the closing time of the

---

15 Money orders are like certified checks. You need to pay the face amount of the money order and a fee to purchase a money order. For regular checks, you cannot withdraw money for the deposited checks until the money arrives in your bank account from the bank from which the checks were drawn. You can also place stop payment orders on regular checks but not on money orders.

store and started comparing the number of money orders against the record of sale. Obviously, there was a shortage of one money order.

I explained what happened to the manager, but he did not seem to believe me right away. He then asked me to find the torn-up money order. By that time, however, the trash had been already collected and the garbage can was empty. He directed me to go to the storage where all garbage bags were stored and to search for it. There were about twenty garbage bags in the storage. I opened and checked every bag but was out of luck. After watching me awhile, the manager told me to stop the search and go home. I apologized to him again and then left the store. When I reported to work the next day, I found out that my duties had changed. I was reassigned to the front counter. For me, it was a demotion, though the pay remained the same. I was still grateful that I was not fired. This episode became a valuable lesson reminding me to be more understanding when an employee in my law office would make a mistake.

My first younger sister worked an overnight shift at a donut shop on weekends while in high school. She was paid around twenty dollars after taxes for a whole night's work. It was not much, but she was pleased that she did not have to ask for any allowance from our parents, who were struggling to keep up with their new immigrant life. She bought what she needed with the money she earned and still managed to save some. When I was in college, she occasionally sent me a letter with a twenty-dollar bill in it. Of course, I was careful in spending that money, knowing well how hard my sister had worked to earn it.

One of the recommendations that I always make to high school students is to hold a part-time job. You need to experience hard work firsthand; only then, can you develop a true understanding for hardworking people and learn that it is not that easy to earn money. One might argue that there would be no time for work for high school students these days as they all maintain busy schedules, but I believe that working a part-time job in lieu of one of their extracurricular activities might be a more valuable experience. I am not saying that you need to be facing financial difficulties. Is there not a proverb that says, "hard work at a young age cannot be bought with money"? Experiencing hard work when you are still a student could become a strong pillar later in life, whatever your job might be. You could also gain valuable financial wisdom on how to budget and use money.

Both of my sons attended Thomas Jefferson High School for Science and Technology and worked full time during summer vacation after their sophomore year. My older son's job was to document all the pictures and the commemorative plaques hung on the walls at a hospital. The younger son worked as a cashier at a restaurant inside a supermarket. They could have taken jobs at large labs if they wanted, but I thought that those kinds of jobs could wait. Instead, my older son learned to be patient from the boredom of simple labor and the second one, who earned the minimum wage, learned the lesson of the value of money. He had to work for more than an hour to earn enough money to have a simple lunch that he could consume in less than five minutes. Of course, standing an entire day and every day at work must not have been easy, but the experience gained was priceless.

I suggest to all parents that they encourage their high school-aged children to hold a hardworking job before graduating. Back when I was an alumnus interviewer for Harvard, I used to view applicants with high school work experience more positively.

Soccer

The Korea Times–Washington, D.C.
October 5, 2012

I have no talent for playing sports. I have a terrible backhand in tennis and ping-pong. I gave up on swimming as I could not float. As for golf, the balls simply would not fly straight. In my high school entrance examination in Korea, two points were deducted from my physical fitness test. Despite my lack of athletic talents, however, I still played soccer with my neighborhood friends until immigrating to the U.S. My friends and I used to play against the teams composed of the older neighborhood brothers or the teams from other neighborhoods with a bet of pastries on the line. Our team often won the bet, thanks to my athletic friends.

I attended George Washington Junior High School during my first year in the U.S. One day, a classmate encouraged me to join a neighborhood soccer team. Soccer was not that popular in Virginia at the time. Surprisingly, I stood out in the team only because the team was not that good.

During the second semester of my first year, my school started a soccer team. The coach must have heard my reputation as a player on my neighborhood team. He asked me to join the school team. Ironically, he was a wrestling coach and had never played soccer in his life. The school assigned him to the soccer team as there was no other suitable candidate.

The team was formed at last, but no one knew where to begin. Out of blue, the coach asked me to oversee the practice sessions. That was how, for the first time in my life, I ended up coaching soccer. Of course, I completely lacked coaching skills. In addition, my poor English made it worse. I had no control over the team. I remember asking the players to just run around the field quite a lot until they all became out of breath.

Finally, the regular season started. In our very first game, I played as the team's center forward—that shows how bad the team was. Toward the end of the first half of the game, one player from the opposing team and I ended up kicking the ball at the same time and I sprained my ankle. I complained about the pain and the coach put in a substitute for me. The pain, however, did not subside even when the second half started, so I had to sit out for the remainder of the game. My sprained ankle did not heal until the end of the season, and my career as a soccer player also ended along with it.[16]

Raising two sons, I got interested in soccer again. They joined the neighborhood soccer teams. I gave them rides twice a week and I cheered for them with full-throated exuberance at every weekend game. I got sucked into my passion for soccer again, the passion that I had long forgotten about. Both of my sons started playing soccer even before entering elementary school and continued to play until high school. Since they had played two seasons each year, spring and fall, it is not an exaggeration for me to claim that we had spent about half of the year every year for fifteen years thinking and talking about soccer.

Then, on one day at the beginning of a spring season during my younger son's fourth grade, I dropped off my son at the soccer field and wanted to watch the practice a little. The team coach was coming late for the practice, so the parents were just letting children play on their own. I could tell that none of the parents had much knowledge about playing soccer.

Just to be helpful, I ran out to the field and began kicking balls with the children in the middle of the field. I forgot that I was wearing dress shoes. The coach finally arrived. He was a young father who worked as a prosecutor for Fairfax County. I learned

---

16 In the following year, I tried out for the soccer team at T.C. Williams Senior High School. The first test was running, and that was where I learned my physical limitations. I was the slowest, and, of course, I did not make the team.

later that he had not volunteered to become the coach. He had never coached previously nor had he even played soccer before. He reminded me somewhat of the wrestling coach who had ended up coaching my junior high school soccer team.

Unable to contain myself, I asked him whether I could help. Even before the coach completed his sentence in thanking me, I found myself running back onto the field. That was how I became an assistant coach. The title was on paper only, and I soon assumed the role of head coach during practices and at the matches. Luckily, our team ended the season with a good record. One regret, though, was how I had treated my own son. I had acted more strictly with him than the other players. I guess that I did not want to be seen by the other players or parents as playing favoritism towards my son. At times, my son seemed disappointed, but he was still proud of his father being the coach.

It is unbelievable that I, a non-athlete, ended up coaching two soccer teams in my lifetime. Those precious memories will remain in my heart forever. I still remember vividly those days on soccer fields whenever I see small children running around on fields. Should I look for a team that might be interested in taking me on as an assistant coach?

Appreciation plaque given to me after the season.
Some players are missing in the picture.

Admission To Harvard

April 2020

It is unbelievable that someone like me could immigrate to the U.S. in the middle of high school and get admitted to Harvard. I believe that my hard work, the support of many people around me, and some luck, all combined, made it possible. I would not have been admitted had any of these been missing.

After completing my sophomore year of high school in Korea, I studied English conversation for a few months at an English academy. Then, in the summer of 1974, I left Korea. In those days, high school English classes in Korea, unlike now, mostly concentrated on reading, learning grammar, and memorizing vocabulary. Listening, speaking, and writing were almost non-existent. The teachers were not prepared to teach them, either. Therefore, my English skills were minimal when I first arrived in the U.S.

After arriving in the U.S., we settled down in the City of Alexandria, Virginia. Alexandria is an old city located just south of the capital city, Washington, D.C. It is adjacent to Fairfax County where I currently live. The city had a large population of African Americans, and the high schools there had finally integrated only a few years prior to my arrival. As a result, the freshmen and sophomores attended George Washington Junior High School (GW) and Hammond Junior High School while all the juniors and seniors attended T.C. Williams High School (TC). A majority of the African American students at T.C. came from GW.

I was old enough to be placed in the junior year, but I decided to enroll as a sophomore because I desperately needed more time to enhance my English language skills before I went to college. So, I enrolled in GW as the apartment that my family lived in was located within its school boundaries. The grades and course credits I earned during my freshman year in Korea were recognized. I was assigned to an English as Second Language (ESL) class. In addition to the ESL class, I was also enrolled in a regular English class, math, chemistry, physical education, world history, and shop classes.

All these classes were held every day. However, the ESL class was not given any credit, and the class period for the ESL changed from day to day. For example, if the ESL class were during the first period on Monday, it would be changed to the second period on Tuesday and then the third period on Wednesday. The reason for changing the class period was to provide the ESL students with opportunities to attend all other regular classes. If ESL class were held during the same period every day, the students would obviously have to miss the regular class held during the same period.

There were only a few immigrant students at GW at the time. In addition to me, the ESL class only had one student each from Thailand, Vietnam, and South America. The range of the students' ages and English skills was wide. The female student from Vietnam was the best in speaking and listening. She had been in the U.S. for the longest. I used to look at her with much envy and wondered when I could ever get to become as good as she was. I was much behind the other students in listening and speaking, but I was not so bad in grammar. I believe that being among other English language learners helped me overcome my fears of being embarrassed from making mistakes and, therefore, also improve my English skills more quickly. The ESL class teacher also allowed the students to attend the regular classes instead of the ESL class whenever they wanted. After the first semester, I rarely went to the ESL class.

I immersed myself in study as I realized that all I could do was to try harder. Listening and speaking were always difficult. And it was hard to comprehend what was being taught in the class. I was confident in math, especially in solving problems. All I had to do was to look up in the dictionary the words in the problems that I did not understand and to decipher the problems. In fact, even back in Korea, I always got good grades in math even without studying. In the math class at GW, however, I used to bother David Rall, who sat in front of me, to ask for help in understanding what was being said in class and in deciphering the math problems.[17]

David Arthur Lloyd Rall in his graduation gown (1977)

I used to poke David's back with the eraser end of my pencil whenever I had a question. Then, one day, I could not find David in his seat. I looked around and saw him sitting in the very first row. He must have moved there to avoid me. I was not willing to give up, so I grabbed my belongings and moved up myself to sit right behind him. I am sure that he thought that I was being ridiculous. After that incident, however, David and I became good friends and got along very well until our graduation. I helped him on math and

17 David entered Johns Hopkins University after high school and studied physics there. He then obtained his Ph.D. in physics from University of Wisconsin and now works for the federal government.

physics, and he helped me with English and American life. David also taught me tennis and often took me to basketball and football games.

To my surprise, the most difficult subject was not English but World History. On top of not being able to comprehend what the teacher was saying, I could not understand the assignments. There were so many difficult words in the textbook, and I could not handle the endless writing assignments. I got a D for my first quarter grade. Perhaps the teacher did not have the heart to give me a failing grade. I was grateful for not getting an F. I decided to study harder and paid more attention to my assignments. I managed to get a C for my second quarter grade. As the third quarter began, I started memorizing the content of the textbook in a desperate attempt to prepare for the tests. I had always had a talent for memorizing since I was young.

Memorizing the textbook content made the essay tests much easier to answer. I just had to transcribe what I had memorized onto the papers. Even the grammar was perfect. Well, you could not write better than the textbook. For example, if a test question asked me to elaborate on the causes for the outbreak of World War II, I wrote down as much as possible from what I had memorized. My grade went up to a B in the third quarter and then finally to an A by the fourth. I was able to achieve a B as the yearend grade after doing well on the final exam.

For English, I started with a C but ended with an A—the final grade was a B. I received As in all other subjects. The math was easy for me. I was good in Chemistry as well. Good attendance and participation almost guaranteed an 'A' for our physical education class. In the shop class, the students learned to assemble vacuum tube radios, build wood products using the woodworking tools, draw blueprints, and such, and I was able to do those as well as any other student. So, I received four As and two Bs for the six regular classes in the first year. With that, the total number of Bs that I had up to that point was three, with the third one coming from my freshman year physical education class from Korea. From junior year on, I had studied at T.C. I received all As in junior year. By the time I arrived at T.C., I did not need to attend ESL class anymore. I survived the most difficult subject, English, by putting in extra effort.

I also joined the math team at T.C. in junior year. There were two teams, one for the juniors and another for the seniors. A math competition was held once a month among the schools in Alexandria. To my recollection, our school was the only public school participating in the competition, with the other two schools being private ones. The private schools sent one team each while T.C. sent two. The results of the competition were always the same every month. The first place went to the senior team and the second place to the junior team of my school.

For the individual recognitions, however, I received the first place at the end of the year, passing all the seniors. The senior team members included those who were admitted to colleges like Yale, MIT, and UPenn, and they were all surprised. And, luckily, my performance on the math team attracted the attention from Dr. William Dunkum, the chairman of the science department at our school.

Dr. William Dunkum teaching in the classroom (1977)
The photo was provided by Alexandria City Public Schools.

Dr. Dunkum taught physics while in charge of the science department. I took his class in junior year, and he considered me to be the top student in his class. I also maintained a special relationship with him. I used to arrive at school early because I got a ride from my father instead of taking the school bus. As his job was in Washington, D.C., my father left home early in the morning to avoid traffic. Sometimes the school's front entrance was not even open when I arrived at the school, so I had to wait for someone to come and open the door. I usually had more than an hour to kill before classes would start.

Dr. Dunkum came to school early, too. He used to be the first one to arrive among the teachers. I always went over to greet him and was also able to have conversation with him. Our conversation topics were not limited to physics, and I had all sorts of questions. I asked him anything that came into my mind in those days. He was kind to give me his full attention, patiently listening to my heavy Korean accent and getting to know me well in the process. After witnessing my outstanding performance on the math team as well as in his physics class, he nominated me for a Governor's School program during the summer break after my junior year. There were three nominees for the Governor's Schools from our school at the time, with one each in the areas of English, art, and math and science. I was the nominee for math and science.

RPI Math & Science Medal

I also received an RPI Math and Science Medal on Dr. Dunkum's recommendation. I believe that this award, along with the recommendation letter I received from Dr. Dunkum, played the most critical role in my admission to Harvard. RPI refers to Rensselaer Polytechnic Institute, located in New York State, a college well known for its excellent engineering programs.

RPI Medals were given to juniors recommended by the participating high schools. Along with the medal, the prizes included an almost guaranteed acceptance to RPI with scholarships for four years based on financial need. I felt grateful to have this acceptance to an excellent college already guaranteed for me even before completing junior year. Therefore, when it was the time for me to apply for colleges in senior year, I decided to try for some of the top colleges in the U.S., such as Harvard, MIT and Caltech. I might not have even dreamed about applying to those colleges had I not been guaranteed acceptance to RPI. At the end of the day, I had received admission offers from all colleges to which I had applied.

As for Harvard, MIT, and Caltech, I had applied for early action. My high school counselor shared with me later about the conversation he had with an admissions officer from Caltech. The admissions officer had told my counselor that he had never seen the kinds of excellent recommendation letters that my teachers had written for me and asked my counselor to persuade me to come to Caltech.[18] I have never seen those recommendation letters myself, so I do not know what they included—but they must have been great, and I am forever grateful to the writers, Dr. Dunkum, Mr. Patrick Welsh, my English teacher, and Mr. Michael Graffeo, my guidance counselor.

---

18 Caltech is a small college where the freshman class only had 240 students at the time. About sixty of them drop out at the end of the freshman year.

With Mr. Michael Graffeo, my high school guidance counselor, when he visited my office in August 2021.

Of course, in my own way, my preparation for applying for colleges was methodical, thorough, and focused. I also had to do everything on my own as my parents were not equipped to give me any advice, and I did not have anyone to guide me through the college application process. For example, I purchased test preparation books to study for SAT and Achievement Tests, equivalent to the current SAT IIs. I made a schedule for myself to go through the entire books and stuck to the schedule no matter what. I thought that the amount of time and effort that I was putting in at the time was nothing compared to my friends back in Korea who were studying for the college entrance examination. My life was still relatively easier than theirs. With much effort, I was able to complete SAT and Achievement Test requirements by the end of junior year. That way, all that I had to do during my senior year was to fill out the application forms and work on the essays.

The most important task in preparing for college applications during my senior year was essay writing. I knew that my writing was not that good. I was not in position to seek help from a professional or my parents, either. After much thought, I decided to pick a topic that could leave a long-lasting impression on the readers to compensate for my poor writing skills. Therefore, I chose "The division of the Korean Peninsula—North and South" as the topic.

In my essay, I argued that it was wrong for the U.S. government to contribute to the division after the end of World War II. The U.S. government might claim that it at least saved a half of the country from communist rule; however, the Korean peninsula issues should have been left for the Koreans alone to decide. The superpowers should not have ignored the sovereignty of a nation and its people. Had the nation not been divided, there would not have been people like my father who had left his hometown in North Korea all by himself and had not seen his mother and younger brothers left there for decades. It is tragic that he had not been allowed to visit his hometown for so long. I do not know what the admissions officers might have thought about the essay, but the essay must have helped the admissions officers learn who I was—both my mindset on the topic and how I processed certain historical events.

Unlike MIT, Caltech, and RPI, which all offered me admissions in early actions, Harvard deferred its decision until the regular decision window. Harvard wanted to see whether my English would improve further. They needed to determine whether my English was good enough for me to study at Harvard. I fully understood their position. One of the requirements for the applicants who were English language learners like me was to take the TOEFL (Test of English as Foreign Language). After taking the TOEFL one more time, I finally received an offer of admission from Harvard in its regular decision.

Once I received the offer from Harvard, however, I then had

to make a tough decision. My father and Dr. Dunkum both wanted me to enroll at MIT and major in engineering. I was also leaning towards MIT, but I could not shake off this lingering desire to go to Harvard, arguably the best college in the world. So, I went to Dr. Dunkum every day and asked him why I should not go to Harvard. Suddenly, one day, Dr. Dunkum relented and told me that it would be okay for me to go to Harvard. Not that I did not want to go to MIT, but his change of heart immediately cemented my heart towards Harvard. I guess Harvard had always been first choice in my mind. My life could have been quite different had I elected MIT. Nevertheless, I have never regretted the decision to this date. It was, in fact, the right decision for me.

Harvard aims to admit students whom it deems worth educating. Harvard must have determined that I had potential to contribute to society with a Harvard education, even though my English language skills were not as good as the other Harvard admittees. Well, Harvard indeed made the right decision in accepting me. I say this with humility that I have become a role model for many students out there—after all, I am one of the few Asian immigrants who have stepped up to serve in public office, now having served for twenty years as an elected school board member working hard to provide and improve public education for all.

My freshman dorm at Harvard (Holworthy Hall).
I lived on the third floor going up from the entrance on the far right.

Mushu Pork

Washington Media
August 6, 2000

It was during my college freshman year in 1977. At the beginning of the year, I befriended a Korean student from New York. One day when his whole family came to visit him, I was asked to join the family for dinner. His family was large and included his parents, an older brother who was a graduate school student at MIT, an older sister in college, and a younger sister and brother who were both in high school—there were eight of us altogether for the dinner. We went to a Chinese restaurant near Harvard Square.

We started ordering food from the menu. I was planning to just to eat whatever they ordered since I was a guest. Honestly, I would not have even known what to order anyway as I had never been to an American-style Chinese restaurant before. An appetizer came out, but I had no clue what it was or how to eat it. I learned later that it was called mushu pork. At the time, the only Chinese foods that I knew were a few Korean-style Chinese foods like jjajangmyeon, udong, jjamppong, fried dumplings, and sweet and sour pork.

I managed to imitate the other people around the table and took a piece of what looked like a Korean mung bean pancake—but I did not know the next step with it. I could have just asked or at least looked around the others. However, I did not. I felt too embarrassed to even hold my head up. I found out later how to eat it: first, spread the sauce on top of the pancake, and then put on mixture of pork and vegetables before wrapping it to eat. While all others ate the mushu pork, I was only tearing off the pancake into small pieces and eating one piece at a time, while keeping my head down the whole time. I could feel everyone peeking at me. There was a dead silence around the table. It felt like the longest dinner ever in my life.

I can laugh about it now, but I was breaking out in a cold sweat that day. Remembering the episode, I sometimes treat my two young sons in elementary school with mushu pork. I also try to take them to different restaurants to give them opportunities to experience various cuisines.[19]

Mushu Pork

I do not want my children to face the same embarrassing moments I did. However, of course, it will be impossible for me to take them to try all the different foods from every country in the world nor is it even necessary. It is more important to teach them to have the courage to ask questions when they encounter a similar situation. It is only natural not to know what to do if you have never learned or experienced something. It is nothing to be ashamed of.

---

19 Among the foods my kids liked a lot include Ethiopian and Indian foods. They also liked kabobs which we often had after the Sunday church service.

Insecurity

The Korea Times-Washington, D.C.
April 14, 2017

According to the personality analysis tests that I have taken, I am an introvert. The first time I saw that test result, I was shocked and doubted its accuracy. I thought that there might have been an error in my results. So, I went through a few more tests, but the results always came back the same. But come to think of it now, the results are correct.

I could not believe the test results at first because of my public persona. I have had a lot of experience standing in front of people and participating in a multitude of events as an elected official. Even prior to coming to the U.S. as a high school student, I often served in leadership positions in school, including being the president of the student government association, and I never had trouble speaking in public to large groups of people. As such, I had always assumed that I must be an extrovert. Of course, this was based purely on my own thoughts and not through any personality analysis test.

The biggest difference between being an extrovert and being introvert is that an extrovert obtains energy by interacting with other people while an introvert does so by reflecting in solitude. In that sense, I would say that it is correct that I am an introvert. Of course, there is no value judgment between the two personalities—they are just two different personalities. As far as leadership is concerned, I believe that anyone can be a leader regardless of his personality type. It is just that more preparation, training, and efforts might be needed for an introvert to be a public figure.

On the other hand, I wonder whether my personality has changed over time. Looking back, I had spent a lot of time alone after immigrating to the U.S. My personality might have changed during the process of trying to adapt to a new life and overcome the challenges posed by language and cultural differences. This period of being alone a lot began immediately after my arrival to the U.S. and continued through college and law school. My lifestyle changed during my first ten years in the U.S. as well. I think that I have learned to gain more strength through meditating rather than necessarily associating with other people.

Throughout most of my first year of high school in the U.S., I had often remained in an empty classroom during lunch and read the Bible alone. This had more to do with my desire to avoid having conversations with other students in the school cafeteria than being a good Christian. If I had been in the cafeteria, I would have had to speak English to communicate with other students since there were almost no other Korean speaking students at school. Conversing in English felt like torture for me at that time.

Things did not get any easier in college. A vast majority of the Korean students at Harvard were either born in the U.S. or had immigrated at an early age; thus, there were huge cultural and language gaps between them and me. So, I ended up hanging out with the Korean students at MIT instead. MIT had quite a few students with backgrounds like mine, and I felt much closer to them. I often visited and spent weekends at MIT.

There was an episode on the very first day of my freshman year at Harvard. When I went to the freshman dining room, I saw the food trays looking like the one in this picture below. The food trays that I had been familiar with until that point were all rectangular in shape. I was confused which side-whether the longer or the shorter-should be close to my body.

I would have figured it out if I had looked around and observed how the other students put down their trays on the tables, but I was too self-conscious and could not look around. I was obsessed with the thought that everyone was watching me. I ended up discreetly turning the tray 180 degrees after each bite of food. I repeated this for a while until I finally gained some courage to look around and to learn that no one was paying attention to me. I also noticed that there seemed to be no rule as to how the trays should be placed on the tables. In fact, there was no correct answer on which way to put down the trays.

I did not have much confidence in myself then, and I still suffer from some of the same insecurity at times even now. Thinking back on those days brings a bitter smile to my face, and I feel a lump in my throat when I think about how many other Koreans, especially young children, might be experiencing similar situations. There may be some students trying to cope with their personalities changing just like I did. Let us look around and see whether we can find any student in need.

With the MIT friends (1979)
I am in the middle with glasses.

Shyness

The Korea Times-Washington, D.C.
March 3, 2011

It was my freshman year in college. I attended a Korean church located about twenty minutes away by car from our campus. I used to get a ride to the church from one of the graduate school students as I did not have my own car. It was a small church with forty to fifty members and with about a dozen people in the church choir. I joined the choir, and on one day after the church service, I was invited by the choir director, who was also the church piano accompanist, to his house for dinner.

The choir director had come to the U.S. as a graduate student and married an American. After the dinner prepared by the choir director's wife, I said a goodbye with thanks to the hosts and headed out to go back to the dormitory. Unfortunately, I did not know exactly where I was on the map. There was a bus stop in front of the house, and I was told to wait for a bus to come by. By the time I got to the bus stop, however, it was already late at night and dark all around. To make matters worse, it started raining. I forgot to check the weather forecast in the morning, so I had not brought an umbrella. I found a shelter near the bus stop and waited patiently for the bus.

Time passed, but the bus never arrived. I found out later that there was no bus on Sunday nights. The choir director did not know the bus schedule as he always drove. After waiting for a couple of hours, I finally decided to hitchhike. It was my first time trying to hitchhike.

The problem was that there was no one willing to give a ride to an Asian stranger wearing a black suit and holding a black Bible without an umbrella on a dark and rainy night. It was so ridiculous to wait endlessly for a bus that never arrived. Anyway, to make a long story short, I finally got a ride around the midnight and returned to school safely. I do not know why I did not go back to the choir director and ask him for a ride. Come to think of it, I guess that I must have felt so embarrassed about myself.

I can laugh about it now, but it was a nerve-wracking experience back then. I thought that I was brave because I had given a lot of presentations in front of people from an early age. However, I sometimes detect my shyness in unexpected situations. I can even detect a similar shyness from my own two sons. I sometimes see them taking a detour from the natural path or just stand there due to silly pride or an embarrassment. It is frustrating to witness my own children in those situations.

However, when giving advice to their children even in those situations, parents would be wise not to directly hurt their pride or cause further embarrassment. Even advice given with good intentions could instead hurt their feelings or trigger a conflict with them.

Career Path Decisions

The Korea Times-Washington, D.C.
September 26, 2014
February 1, 2019
Updated: May 2021

I had an opportunity to give lectures at two high schools on my visit to Korea in the autumn of 2018. Sharing my life stories and experiences, I challenged the students to pursue their passion. A question-and-answer session followed, and I still cannot forget the two questions brought up at one school.

One student stated, "I have heard that passion alone does not lead to a successful life these days." That was obviously a comment, but also a question thrown at me. The student seemed to be asking whether we would not need money, power, family influence, and good educational background to achieve what people consider to be a successful life—a sharp comment and not an easy question to answer.

I responded to her that it would depend on how to measure success. If the focus were to maximize your own profit, then surely passion alone might not be enough. However, if it were to become a valuable person to others, then your life could still be successful even without the other elements that the student had mentioned. I was not sure whether anyone was convinced by my response and started wondering what students would consider to be success in life.

Another question was what I would have done had I remained in Korea rather than immigrating to the U.S. That was another tough question. I did not remember having clear conviction or a dream of what I wanted to do with my life when I was living in Korea. Many high school students with interest in humanities or social sciences in my generation typically aimed to study law in college and then become a judge or prosecutor after passing the bar exam. I would most likely have followed the same path if I had stayed in Korea. I left Korea to come to the U.S. before seriously thinking about the career path that I wanted to pursue. Therefore, I responded that I was not sure what I would have become. Thinking about that question, I still wonder sometimes what I would be doing right now if I were in Korea.

At various times over the years prior to entering law school, I had contemplated several different career paths. When I entered college, I thought about majoring in chemistry only because I had studied and had done well in chemistry for three years in high school. I quickly realized after my first semester in college that chemistry was not for me—that organic chemistry class was a killer.

So, I ended up changing my major to East Asian Studies. I sensed that it was just a matter of time before China would become a world power. I thought about focusing my studies on China, majoring in international relations in graduate school, and then eventually becoming a diplomat. I also had this grand vision of returning to Korea and contributing my talent to the rebuilding of my home country. That was why I took a gap year in college and went to Taiwan to study Chinese.

However, after I returned to the U.S. from Taiwan and began my senior year of college, I began to rethink my future. I even considered going to a seminary at one point, but that idea got quickly buried when the senior pastor of the church that I was attending advised me that I could better serve the Lord as a layman. What he truly meant to say was that I lacked the requisite qualities to become a pastor. Well, he was right. At the last minute, I decided to go to law school. I comforted myself with a reminder that I would have applied to study law in college if I had been still living in Korea as well. That was the excuse and rationale behind my decision to go to law school.

For about ten years after law school, I had only concentrated on my law practice. Then, for the next twenty-five years, I had carried on careers in both law and public service—I had spent twenty and a half years as a school board member and four years as a planning commissioner.

My first son Joonyoung singing with his Christian a cappella group.[20]

Let me share my two sons' career paths. The older son majored in economics at Harvard. He worked as a consultant for the federal government for three years after graduation. He then wanted to work for a non-profit organization, a dream that he had held since his college years. He first went to India for a few months to experience life in an underdeveloped country, and after returning from India, he then went to work for a non-profit foundation for about three years, focusing his efforts on environment, agriculture, and public

20 He liked music so much that he sang with the group and played in orchestra during his freshman and sophomore years, but he had to give up orchestra during his junior and senior years as he needed to focus on his role as the music director for the a cappella group.

health. As he felt the need to study more, he then went to UC Berkeley for a master's degree in public policy. He is currently working in state government in a food aid program for poor residents.

My son shared with me a story about the conversation he once had with his roommates when he was in college. That is a story that I proudly share with other people from time to time. Sitting in the living area of their dorm suite, he and his roommates exchanged their aspirations for the future. One roommate shared his dream of making a lot of money quickly. He was going to work on Wall Street and become a millionaire in a couple of years after graduating from college. Another roommate declared that he would enter the political world. He wanted to run and become a congressman and a U.S. Senator, and he would even run for President if an opportunity arose.

It then became my son's turn to share his goals in life. He first told his roommates that he would pray for their dreams. He wanted them to become rich and politically influential. He then put them on notice that he would come back and ask them to please help him with their money and political influence as he was going to work for a non-profit organization. His non-profit organization would certainly be able to use their money and power. My son does not consider money-making as important for himself. He has always wanted his talent utilized to help the people in need, and he is currently on the right track.

My second son, on the other hand, received his doctoral degree in physics from the University of Illinois at Urbana-Champaign (UIUC) in the spring of 2019. He had received his bachelor's degree from Brown. His doctoral research projects changed a couple of times during his six years at UIUC. He started out with condensed matter and then moved onto high energy particle physics, even going to Switzerland for a semester to research high energy particle physics. However, he ended up changing gears to biophysics and went into a cancer research using big data. He expressed a desire to work in a big data related field and ultimately in AI (artificial intelligence) development. At one point, he even considered going to medical school.

His first job after graduate school was to work as a data science engineer at a small tech company where he had a summer internship the previous year. After staying there for nine months, he was recruited to come to work as an applied scientist for one of the largest companies in the world on projects like the research work that he had done while in the graduate school. After about a year into his second job, he then transitioned again to work for another tech startup, this time as an AI researcher.

When I look back on myself and my sons, I feel that making decisions on one's career path can be difficult. Identifying the most suitable work for oneself is not going to come easily. You may never know whether a particular career or job would fit you unless you do the work. We hear that young people these days often change their jobs and even their career paths. My hope for them is that no matter what they do, they would do it with passion and focus on being beneficial to others rather than on selfish desires. I also hope that they will measure their success by how positively they are influencing other people's life.

Let us also remember that it is not helpful or even realistic to expect young students to finalize their decisions on future career paths before going to college. They should not even be forced to decide what to major in before they are ready. They need to take their time and not rush these types of decisions. Fortunately, Harvard did not require me to declare my major prior to coming to Harvard and allowed students to change their majors up until the second semester of their sophomore years; hence, I was able to change my major to a social science from the natural sciences.

According to some statistics, Americans change their careers five to seven times in their lifetime, and about one-third of people change jobs each year. In other words, you may have changed your job about ten times by the age of forty-two. Therefore, it is entirely all right for someone to have second thoughts on their career path, and they should not be bothered by such changes. Neither the young people nor their parents should be too anxious about this.

Chapter 2

Raising Two Children

I received a card from my older son, born in 1988, on Father's Day a few years ago. This card marked a significant moment where I learned of the positive impact I had, and continue to have, as he grows and continues to build his life. He, like myself, graduated from Harvard and was planning to get married last year; however, due to the pandemic, the wedding was postponed for a year at first and then subsequently canceled.[21] Challenges like this will come, but I am proud to see both of my sons face them with perseverance.

Although I always tried my best in raising my two children, there were areas where I lacked adequate parenting skills. I always hoped to be a father of whom my children could be proud, but our relationships did not always follow the path I intended while my children were growing up. We sometimes had arguments and even engaged in psychological battles at times.

I framed the card I received from my elder son and prominently display it in my study. I really cherish this card. In the card, he stated that he learned the true meaning of how to love the three things that he considered truly mattered the most in his life—God, family, and the world—all from me. He also wrote that the values I had instilled in him had become the center of his life and that he hoped to pass them on to his own children. I was so touched. At the same time, I also felt relieved that I had done a decent job in raising my children well after all. Thank you, Joonyoung and Wooyoung. I really love you very much!

---

21 Finally, he was able to get married on the front lawn of Cambridge City Hall in May of 2021 with only three family members as guests. The bride's family watched the wedding on Zoom from out of the country.

Dear 아빠,

6-16-16

Happy Father's Day! I just wanted to let you know how much I appreciate all that you've done for me and that I realize I've come to learn a lot about becoming a man from you. I know that I have probably been a little difficult at times over the past handful of years, and I want to apologize for that. It has taken me some time to grow up and reflect on my life and what truly matters to me - God, family, the world - you have shown me throughout my life what it means to love all of those. Of course, as I blaze my own path, things may look a little different, but the values you instilled in me will be core to who I am and what I hope to pass onto my own family when the time comes (not yet, so don't get too excited!) Hope you have a great Father's Day and enjoy these awesome chocolates! You're supposed to let it melt on your tongue for a bit before chewing apparently!

Love,
Joonyoung

The Two Sons

Washington Media
February 10, 1999
The Korea Times-Washington, D.C.
August 31, 2010
April 6, 2018

The age gap between my two children is three and a half years. I can confidently say that I did not play favoritism between them. They have always been remarkably close to each other. However, I am sure that there were times when the older one might have felt that I favored his younger brother.

My older son was the first grandchild in the family, so he was doted on by everyone since his birth. Everything he had done became the core conversation topic for his grandparents, aunts, and uncles. Then my younger son was born. The older one soon found out that all the attention and love he had been accustomed to receiving now had shifted to the baby. He must have felt betrayed, hard to bear for a three-year-old.

He was too young to understand the concept of "a younger brother" when his brother was born. Fortunately, he did not harm the baby although it must have been difficult to control his emotion at times. That is not to say that he was never bothered by the existence of a younger sibling. One day, he offered a suggestion about whether we should not leave the baby in the woods. I told him that there were scary animals like the tigers or the wolves in the woods. He seemed to be thinking about it for a moment and then asked again whether we could not then find the woods where deer and rabbits lived. That conversation made me realize that I needed to give the older son more attention.

When my younger son was around three or four years old,

every time he saw his mother and older brother sitting side by side, he would squeeze in between them and forcefully push out his brother. The younger one normally slept with his mom at night, and he had a habit of rubbing his mom's cheeks with his hands. His older brother occasionally tried to squeeze in between them but had never been successful. He would get kicked out by his younger brother in less than ten seconds. Surely, the younger one would not have won against his older brother if based on strength alone. But the older one always acted defeated at the younger one's persistent effort, with his unpleasant feelings hidden in an uncomfortable laughter.

Watching them, I was proud of the older one yielding to his younger brother without a fight. However, I regret now that I did not remind them at that time that the older one also had equal rights to sit beside his mom and sleep with her at night. After all, the older one was only six or seven years old and still a child himself.

Joonyoung (born 1988) and Wooyoung (born 1991)
in front of the house

Both of my two sons signed up for neighborhood soccer teams. I used to join them for practice in our front yard. I would throw the ball to them alternately so that they could practice trapping the ball—the skill of controlling an incoming soccer ball against the ground. I would then give them scores on their trapping skills. Both boys wanted to receive good scores from me, but they also wanted to outperform each other. The younger one was incredibly competitive and did not want to lose to his older brother. At each throw, he wanted to get a higher score.

To speak the truth, I did not throw the balls fairly. I threw the balls in a way that it would be more difficult for the older one to trap the ball. I did that because not only was there an age gap requiring a tougher throw to the older one, but, most of all, the younger one had to win; otherwise, he would end up crying. Of course, I'm sure the older one would also have liked to get a higher score and win the competition as well. I admit that my one-sided thought that the older one should give way to his younger brother was short-sighted.

My older son was also more considerate of other people than his younger brother. It must not have been easy being so all the time. Their grandfather sometimes would take them to a nearby toy store to buy them toys. The younger one would often end up picking an expensive toy. However, the older son would worry about their grandfather's spending money, so he would choose a cheaper one ever after initially considering more expensive ones. As the younger boy would pick whatever he wanted without caring much about the price, the older boy would sometimes lecture his younger brother for choosing an expensive toy.

The younger son would then protest to his older brother that it was not the older brother but rather their grandfather who was paying for the toys. After overhearing their quarrel, their grandfather would tell the older one that it would be okay for him to choose a more expensive toy as well, but the older boy would not change his mind. He had matured too early. I feel a lump in my throat whenever I think about what he must gone through whenever he had to restrain himself from doing what he wanted to do. I am sure that he, just like any other child, would have also wanted to get more expensive toys.

There was another incident when my younger one was in his sophomore year of college. I planned to give him a ride back to school. During his freshman year, he had lived with a white roommate who had brought a small fridge. However, for sophomore year, he had decided on renting a place with a group of Korean students and was uncertain whether anyone would bring a fridge. A small fridge was not that expensive, so I decided to purchase a new one for him so that he could use it for three years until he would graduate from college.

However, upon hearing of my plan for a new fridge, my older son disagreed with me and recommended purchasing a secondhand one. He said that I could buy one at a much cheaper price from other students. I explained to him that students normally would sell their belongings at the end of the school year when they would have to vacate their dorm rooms—it would be difficult to find one at the beginning of the year. Also, a new fridge was not expensive at all. Yet he kept insisting that I should buy a used one.

Eventually, I got annoyed with his insistence and dismissed him to not interfere as the fridge was for his younger brother and not for him. To my dismay, he reacted sharply. He must have been surprised and disappointed by my abrasive retort. I had to control my temper to avoid any unnecessary conflict with him. A thought then raced through my head. I realized that I had never bought him a new fridge during the four years while he had been in college. I do not believe that his sharp reaction was necessarily for that reason, but nevertheless, I still really felt bad for him.

As I mentioned earlier, I tried not to play favoritism while raising two sons, but when someone once asked me whom I felt more bonded with, I remember answering that it was the younger one. I am not saying that I love my older son any less. It is perhaps because I have felt the older to be more reliable and gave me less to worry about when compared to his younger brother who has been a handful, being the younger child.

Looking back, I have many regrets towards the younger one, too. In comparison to the older son to whom we had paid so much attention because everything was the first time in his case, the younger son never received that same kind of dedicated attention. There are significantly fewer videos or the pictures of the younger son. The older one always got the new clothes while many of my younger one's clothes were hand-me-downs from his older brother.

We held a large party inviting many people for the older one's first birthday celebration, but the younger one's was celebrated just with our family members. It was not our intention to give a preferential treatment to the first born. However, by the time the younger one came along, we were lower on energy and thought that celebrating in moderation was a way to show our maturity as parents. There were many other incidents like this one that made me feel sorry towards the younger son.

The boys were competitive with each other while growing up. It was only natural for the younger one to not be able to keep up with his older brother when they were young. They both used to play chess, and the younger one would end up crying each time when he lost a game to his older brother, claiming that his brother was unfair to him. He often complained that his brother's game manner was not good because he never allowed him to take back moves and would even hum during the game. But we always knew that the true reason behind his complaint was nothing more than his frustration from losing. The older son just seemed to enjoy the whole situation.

They would also point out at least one mistake each other made after playing soccer or basketball games. To everyone's surprise, the younger one once received a prize higher than his older brother's from a Korean speech contest. I remember that the younger one's delight and the older one's disappointment both lasted for a long time. Notwithstanding their competitiveness, however, they have grown up as good brothers.

One time, the older son had to take a pre-qualification test for a summer program when he was in the fifth grade. I dropped him off at the test site and then went to watch the younger one's basketball game. The younger son was in the second grade at the time. After the basketball game, I was going back to the test site to pick up the older son along with the younger one.

On our way, the younger one suddenly said that he hoped that his brother would fail the test. I had this sinking feeling. I knew very well about their rivalry, so I often reminded them about and emphasized the importance of always helping each other. Therefore, it was a shock to hear the younger son's comment. I tried to hide my shock and asked him why. To my surprise, his answer was not what I had anticipated. He answered my question with a question of his own: with whom would he play if his brother went away from home for a whole month during the summer? He added that it would be too boring without his brother. It was a moment of relief to know that those two boys were after all brothers who wanted and needed each other.

We tried our best as parents, lest our two intriguingly competitive sons should feel any parental favoritism when they were growing up. Then again, there were times when we made mistakes. For example, there were instances where we would praise or scold one son but not the other in similar situations. Also, we would encourage one to read books or practice the musical instrument but failed to say anything to the other. We should have applied the same rules for both sons equally so that no one would feel being picked on or left out. We sometimes made mistakes, as we did not always think through the possible consequences before taking an action.

Raising the two boys is now irreversibly in the past. They are now old enough to get married themselves and have their own kids. Yet I wish that I could just go back to old days and start all over again. With a second chance, I am sure that I would do a better job My heart is full of regrets.

Having a good time with Joonyoung

Aggressive Parents

Washington Media
September 15, 2000
The Korea Times-Washington, D.C.
March 9, 2012

One of the challenges that I had to face as a member of the school board was dealing with complaints from parents. One thing that you can easily detect in a highly educated and high-income area such as Fairfax County is the high expectations that parents have for their children's education.

The aggressiveness of some parents is remarkable as well. In addition to "tiger" and "helicopter" moms, there are parents who would like to intervene in every aspect of the operation of the schools themselves. There are also many parents who relentlessly fight tooth and nail whenever they feel that their children are being negatively affected. Sometimes, matters even escalate to the school board for a solution when teachers or principals were not able to resolve the issue themselves.

They start with innocuous pleas, but then often devolve into blaming, heckling, and even threatening. Of course, there always are parents trying to intimidate school board members, wielding their voting power as a weapon. They promise to "remember you" at the next election. The complaints are quite varied—they include the amount of homework, relationships with other classmates, quality of the food at the school cafeteria, school bus delays, their child not making the school sports teams, casting for a drama or a musical production, insufficiency of class change times, overcrowded classes, and school facilities, to name but a few.

Many of these parents are highly acclaimed professionals themselves such as lawyers, doctors, college professors, researchers, consultants, military officers, and senior federal government officials. They are all armed with very carefully thought-through logic and analyses to trap the board members. They drain your time and energy and test your mental toughness. That being said, these parents also play a big role in ensuring high quality education and a healthy educational environment in Fairfax School Public Schools. Not only are their arguments often justified, but they are also valuable volunteers in and out of schools. It is true that they complain; however, they also roll up their sleeves and enthusiastically participate whenever there is a need at the school.

To be honest, I used to be one of those parents myself. I do not intend to brag about it, but I also do not feel ashamed of or deny the fact. On the contrary, you are abandoning your job as parents if you fail to be proactive in advocating for your child's rights and interests.

It was when my younger son was in elementary school. One day, he complained about his teacher. He and his classmates worked on the same extra credit project, but he did not get the credit he thought was promised while his classmates did. He objected to the teacher, but the teacher not only simply ignored him, she also did not even look at him with her eyes fixed on a computer screen. He added that the teacher would have scolded him if had he acted in the same way she had done. He thought that the teacher was being rude.

Upon hearing these complaints from my younger boy, I first contacted the principal and requested for a meeting with the teacher. The principal wanted to be present at the meeting as well. At the meeting, I did not hesitate to point out that teachers should lead by example. Of course, teachers have both rights and duties to correct and even discipline bad behaviors of students, but it is also wrong for a teacher not to follow her own teaching. I am sure that the teacher was quite embarrassed to hear such things from a parent, especially more so in the presence of her principal. I knew that I might be considered impolite to address the teacher in that way; however, I felt it necessary so that she would remember not to repeat the same behavior toward her students.

Another incident happened when my older son was in the seventh grade. It was the first Friday after the school year started. My older son forgot to bring his lunch to school, so I brought a lunch to school for him. As I did not know where his classroom was, I decided to check in the main office first.

By coincidence, I met the assistant principal in charge of the seventh graders there. We had known each other since I had first been elected to the school board. Greeting me warmly, he wanted to tell me a funny story involving my older son that had happened in the morning on that day. My son was apparently mistaken by a school security officer as the culprit of some mischief caused by another student. As I was in a hurry to return to work after delivering the lunch, I did not ask him for further details. I cut the conversation short, but my curiosity lingered on.

However, when I later asked my son about the incident, I no longer found the story funny. According to my son, the security officer came into his classroom during the first period and called him to come outside and then asked what he had done during the physical education class the day before. My son listed all the activities as much as he could remember.

When the security officer asked him if there were any strange things happened, my son said no. Then the officer began accusing him of lying. My son told him that he was not lying, but he was told that he or his parents could be fined for it. My son could not believe what he was being told and asked the security officer what the problem was. The officer then accused him of having pulled down his pants and shown the bare butt to a group of girls outside of the girls' locker room. My son insisted that he had not done this and suggested the security officer ask a classmate who could vouch for him. However, the security officer refused to hear him out and grilled him, saying not to get smart with him. Of course, it was revealed later that it was indeed not my son who had pulled the stunt but another student with the same last name.

After listening to the story of the episode, the actions of the security officer were entirely inappropriate. There should be a common courtesy displayed, even to young students. His choice of words of "how dare you pull that shit on me" was unacceptable. My son was not angry, but still felt the whole incident completely was absurd. He expressed that it was the first he had heard such language from an adult directed towards him and found it incredulous that an adult would utter such language at all.

I had to ponder whether to let it pass by or file a complaint to the school. My status as a former school board member at the time gave me some pause before I decided on whether or not to take an action. After much thought, I had to be a parent first and wrote a letter to the seventh-grade assistant principal. A phone call from the principal requesting for a meeting came a couple of days later. The principal, the head school security officer, and the security officer my son had to deal with were all at the meeting.

At the meeting, I stated that as I had already mentioned in my complaint letter to the school, anyone could make a mistake; however, an apology should follow the mistake and verbal abuses should never be allowed in any circumstances. Adults should be polite to students as much as they would want to be respected by their students. Everyone agreed with me that schools must set a good example.

At first, I was worried that my action might rock the proverbial boat. But, at that point, I was more concerned that my son might continue to be afraid of the security officer whenever he saw him in the school if I did not deal with the situation sternly. School security officers act as counselors for the students seeking advice whenever necessary; therefore, they should be always approachable. Relationships between security officers and students should not have any roadblocks.

Both incidents mentioned above happened when I was not a school board member. I acted just like any other aggressive parent would in advocating for their children. To do that, I needed a strong heart and willingness to endure the associated stress.

I do not have any regrets on my actions, although I questioned myself whether there was not a smarter way to have handled the situations.

Advocating for your children's best interest is a parent's solemn duty. Parents should not hesitate to protest when their children are treated unfairly in any way. If language is a barrier, you should bring an interpreter or request for an interpreter to be provided by school. Please do not leave the matters in the hands of the school alone. Parents need to be full partners with schools in looking after their children. Schools expect that from parents and appreciate such parental participation.

Palbulchul (A Fool)

Washington Media
October 13, 1999

In Korea, we call a person bragging about his wife a palbulchul. But, for once, I would like to be that palbulchul today. I attend the Korean United Methodist Church of Greater Washington. Our church held its forty-eighth anniversary worship service last Sunday. A few Koreans living in the Washington, D.C. area, concerned about the future of their home country during the Korean War, had decided to establish a church. Thirty-two people attended the very first worship service, and it has been forty-eight years since then.[22]

The anniversary service was in the format of musical worship. The first and the third worship services at our church are conducted in Korean. The choir members from those two services had rehearsed together for several months to prepare for the anniversary music service. The songs that the choir members practiced but could not sing at the service due to time constraints were recorded separately so that CDs the choirs were going to produce and sell could contain all the songs. The proceeds from the sales were going to be used for mission purposes.

The singing skills were not particularly high as most of the choir members were volunteer amateur singers; however, despite the amateur status of its musicians, the CD contained their heartfelt praises to God. Once CDs become available, I will certainly keep one in the car and listen to the songs over and over while driving.

---

22 The first service was held on October 14, 1951, at the Foundry United Methodist Church in Washington, D.C. For more information, please go to www.kumcgw.org.

I had listened to another CD for a long time last year—it contained Mendelssohn's oratorio St. Paul which the choir had practiced for two years to produce the CD in English.

However, there was one disappointment. My wife, who had rehearsed with the choir all along as the accompanist, was unable to play at the music service. It was because she injured her right pinky just a week prior to the service. One morning, she was getting ready to give a ride for our two sons to the school bus stop. She was putting on her shoes with her right hand holding onto the car door that was open. Our younger son, a third grader, suddenly shut the door hard. Her right hand got jammed between the doors and her right pinky was fractured. She was told later that the nail would fall off and it would take at least four weeks of therapy for her fractured finger to heal.

Despite her injury, she managed to drop off the kids at the school bus stop and came back home. Then she calmly contacted the doctor. I usually become calmer when faced with a difficult situation, but my wife's demeanors on that morning had surpassed my standard.

It was not difficult to imagine how anxious my younger son might have been throughout that day. I asked my wife to make sure that he felt at ease when he came back from school, but again, I was told by my wife that she had already reassured him several times not to worry about it, as it was an accident. People could easily get angry in similar situations; however, my wife was not angry at all.

She first had an x-ray taken and then went to see an orthopedic surgeon accompanied by a family friend who was also a physician. I was told by that friend how calm my wife had remained throughout the whole ordeal without showing any sign of worries. That was truly remarkable of her and I could not help but feel emotional upon hearing it. I am sure that the constant pain in her finger and the setback in the plan to perform with the choir must have been quite unpleasant. Yet she stayed calm throughout so that the people around her would not worry. I was overwhelmed with thoughts of her hiding her pain and disappointment in consideration of others.

My younger son camc out and greeted me when I returned home from work that evening. He must have been nervous for the whole day thinking I may be angry with him. He seemed relieved after I gave him a hug and asked whether he had a good day. My gesture was seen as a confirmation to him that I was not angry. I could sense his tender heart although he normally acted tough and naughty on the surface. I felt sorry for him when thinking about how his day might have been. After all, he was still a child. He was back to his normal self once he realized that neither parent was angry with him. He ran up and down the stairs and all over the house distracting everyone. However, he did not completely forget about the incident. When he went to sleep lying next to his mother, he asked whether he had ever had an accident. His mom's injury was still on his mind.

My wife will still be unable to play piano for a few more weeks, but this accident gave me an opportunity to confirm about and be thankful for her character.[23] It also gave me a chance to reflect upon how I should be more careful not to hurt my two young kids' feelings.

23 She received a doctoral degree in piano performance in the U.S. and has been teaching piano at a public performing arts high school in Washington, D.C. for more than 30 years.

Six Weeks

The Korea Times–Washington, D.C.
August 10, 2010

If you asked me when the longest and most boring six weeks in my life was, I would say that it was four years ago when my younger son went to a summer music camp after his high school freshman year. He was not thrilled about going to the music camp at first, but since his older brother had also already attended the summer music camp at the same age, he could not use his brother as an excuse, leaving for the camp with his violin without much complaint.

He might have thought that it could be exciting to spend six weeks all alone in another state without any family around. He started learning violin from the third grade. Before picking up the violin, he first took some piano lessons from his mother, a piano teacher, but soon gave it up. His brother was learning to play cello at the time after having unsuccessfully tried piano, so he wanted to copy his older brother and play cello too, but his mother and the older brother both suggested for him to try his own instrument instead. His mother also thought that violin would fit his personality better.

Honestly, however, I did not realize that the six weeks without him would feel like forever to me. I did not feel the same when my older son went to a summer camp even for a longer eight-week period, but, strangely, I missed the younger one very much. I still do not know whether it was because he was the youngest.

I checked the calendar every day and impatiently waited for the six weeks to end. It was even harder to wait than back when I used to count the days till our next dates when dating my wife. Maybe it was the so-called "downward flow of parental love" going to the younger son. Or was it a feeling of emptiness from the absence of the youngest? As I was recently reflecting on the good old times of how I missed him those six weeks (now going into his sophomore year in college this fall!), my heart began aching with thoughts of my father.

My father was a refugee who escaped from North Korea in December 1950 during the Korean War. He was only seventeen years old at the time. His hometown was Haeju, Hwanghae Province. My grandfather used to be a teacher and a violin player, but the grandfather passed away when my father was only eight years old. Therefore, my father lived most of his childhood with his widowed mother and two younger brothers. His family was not well off, and he needed to help his mother sell rice cakes. He could not go to middle school right away after graduating from elementary school. He waited for two years before enrolling in middle school, at the same time with his younger brother.

During the early phase of the war, he was able to avoid being sent to the battlefield because he was a good student and was therefore considered "valuable" in restoring the republic after the war—it would be more useful for him to stay alive. However, as the Chinese army intervened in the war, the tables turned, forcing the South Korean military and UN forces to retreat to the south. His mother became worried about her eldest son's safety and urged him to go south with them. As the retreat of the South Korean and UN forces was announced to be temporary and strategic, my father believed that his being away from home would be brief—the retreat, however, became permanent. He ended up facing many near-death situations and had to endure the cold and hunger until he finally reached a relatively safe place.

Sixty years have passed since then.[24] During those years, his life has led him to a marriage, work in Vietnam as a civilian technician, immigration to the U.S. with an American dream, raising three children, and enjoying five grandchildren. But

24 As of 2021, it has now been 71 years.

through all this, he has been patiently and painfully waiting and hoping for the day he might be able to go back to his hometown in North Korea, even though his family's whereabouts there are unknown.

We tried to contact and wrote letters to organizations promoting North-South Korean family reunions multiple times; however, there has been no response yet to this date. It is heartbreaking to hear my father questioning himself in dejection whether he has not been contacted because there is no good news for him. He sometimes laments that the possibility of his family's survival is almost none, considering the famine and the low-quality medical care provided for people in North Korea. However, I still sense that he is not letting go of his hope, holding onto a thin strand of faith.

My grandfather who passed away at the age of twenty-eight in North Korea.

I cannot imagine how my father has withstood the separation from his family for the past sixty years when I could not barely tolerate the six weeks of separation from my son. I am completely torn up now. The division in Korea is a tragedy. This kind of tragedy should never occur anywhere on earth. Reunification of separated families is desperate and imperative as the number of survivors is decreasing fast. Ideology, politics, and economy are all not as important.

I hope that my father can visit and step on the ground in his hometown in the near future. When that time comes, this foolish son who could not even stand the separation for a mere six weeks from his boy, will personally escort his father, who had to endure the sixty years of agony, to his hometown.

Dad, It's O.K.!

Washington Media
November 10, 1999

"Dad, it's O.K." That was what my first son told me when I went into his room to wake him up. It was the morning after the election. I did not have a chance to talk to my sons on the election night as I had come home extremely late. Unfortunately, I had not won this time around.

As I was a hero in their mind, my sons must have been disappointed in the outcome of the election. I was all prepared to tell him that failures could happen in life and that the important thing was to take the experience of a failure and turn it around to make an opportunity for self-development—but even before I could do so, my sixth grader son consoled me first. I could not say anything when I heard, "It's O.K.", except for telling him to go back to sleep more.

I had another chance to talk to my sons that evening and the older one was again trying to outmaneuver me. He said that it was better now that I would have more time to play sports, like soccer, baseball, and basketball, with him after school. He further said that he would outperform me. I joked that it would be difficult for him to shoot the basketball if I blocked him standing right in front of his face because I was still taller. He responded that there was no problem because he was much faster and could run around me and shoot. I promised him a match soon. My wife welcomed the idea that I now could take over giving rides to the children so that she could finally enjoy some time to herself. She also felt relieved that she would not have to see me all stressed out from the endless school board work and the hectic schedule that I used to maintain.

The result of last week's election was unexpected. All the local newspapers had publicly endorsed me ahead of the election. The Fairfax Education Association, the largest teachers' union, had also endorsed me. I had sufficient campaign funds and enjoyed greater name recognition being an incumbent board member. No one doubted my victory. But I lost the election by seven percent. I need to take time to thoroughly analyze what happened, but as of now, I am still at a loss for words on how to explain the outcome. I would like to thank and apologize to all the friends and supporters who have helped me. They must be disappointed with the result, too. I am disappointed as well, but I will take this defeat as a fuel for further growth.

The two electoral cycles that I have gone through, the first one four years ago and now this year's, have opened my eyes on politics. I now have a much better understanding of how to prepare for elections. No matter how good your qualifications and achievements are, they could be useless if they do not lead to votes at the polls.

It is draining on you, both physically and mentally, to run for office. You get to experience the feeling of being on a downward spiral several times a day, thinking about the possibility of a loss, especially when election day is fast approaching: how embarrassing it might be if the results are not good; the depression and guilt I would feel towards the many supporters; the possibility of sinking into further despair and self-pity of feeling worthless; what I would do with all of the free time that would suddenly become available once leaving office—all these thoughts race through your mind.

There is another cruel consequence from facing defeat in an election. Those constant, numerous phone calls I used to receive from constituents will suddenly stop. There is no rationale for a constituent to call the loser to complain about issues. All phone calls will now be re-directed to the winner, who now has the power to address the issues brought up. A lame-duck—that is exactly what I am. To tell the truth, even if it were me as the constituent, I would not make a phone call to a member of the school board with only two months of the term left and soon to be powerless.

However, with all that being said, I can still proudly say that I have carried out all my duties with dignity for the past four years as the first Asian-American elected official in Fairfax County. Of course, some might say that I could have done better. But I believe I have done my best within my ability, and every moment has been precious. Everyone, not just whites or blacks, seemed to have looked at me with the wonder how an Asian could be elected. I could even detect the sense of astonishment from the faces of Asian students, including many Koreans. Most of all, it is so rewarding to become a living example to prove that we all can and should participate in building our community together, regardless of our racial backgrounds. I would like to thank everyone for the support and advice extended to me so that I could have had this invaluable opportunity to serve for the last four years.

Bulgogi Deopbap (Rice Bowl)

The Korea Times-Washington, D.C.
April 6, 2011

My younger son was home last week for his spring break. It was his first visit in two months since he had gone back to college in January after his winter break. I was bustling around to get ready for his arrival, cleaning the house and filling up the refrigerator with food. However, every time he heads back to college, I always get the feeling that I could have done more for him while he was in town.

I thought about back when I was in college myself. Somehow, the more I got used to life in college, the more foreign I felt at my own home. Of course, at home, I could always enjoy homemade meals prepared by my mother, and everyone tried to make me feel comfortable and allow me to get a good rest. However, I ended up not feeling as comfortable at home because a voice in the back of my head was somehow telling me that the school was where I should be as a student. I also felt like I had left some unfinished business at school. This uneasy feeling increased as I advanced through my college years.

Remembering how I felt thirty years ago, I believed that my son would not feel any differently. Regardless of how well parents treat their children, the children will eventually live an independent life when they grow up. It is therefore not strange for the children to think that their parents' house is not the place where they can stay forever.

My second son is not particularly fluent in Korean. Of course, it is not anything to brag about. His vocabulary is limited, and the pronunciations can also be hilarious at times. For example, we recently went to a Korean restaurant where the name of the restaurant was written as *Cheogajip* in English. We all laughed when he pronounced it as "*chi-o-ga-jip*"—not that he would not have known the meaning of cheogajip even if he had pronounced it correctly. Also, it would have been quite difficult for him to understand that ga and jip had the same meaning.

Listening to his awkward pronunciation, I remembered an episode from when he was in high school. He once worked as a cashier at a restaurant inside a supermarket during the summer after his sophomore year. Standing at the front cashier, he would take orders from customers and verbally relay them to the kitchen. Once the food was ready, it would be brought up to the front counter. He would then take the money from the customer and hand over the food. The restaurant where he worked served both Korean and Chinese foods, and it so happened that the chef's English was not that great as he had recently come to the U.S. from Korea. Given that my son's Korean was also not that good, it was therefore just a matter of time until a communication breakdown would occur.

One day, my son came home after a huge argument with the chef over a food order. He said that the chef became angry at him for putting a wrong order, but, according to my son, it was the chef who had misunderstood the order. So, he became angry himself and talked back at the chef. The dish that led to an argument was *bulgogi deopbap*.

A customer requested the dish to be without *pa*. He called out to the chef, "*bulgogi deopbap* without *pa*." *Bulgogi* is marinated barbecued beef; *deop*, cover; *bap*, cooked rice; and, *pa*, green onion in Korean. Therefore, *bulgogi deopbap* is *bulgogi*-covered-rice. However, instead of not having *pa*, the dish came out without *bap*. The chef must have heard the *pa* as *bap*. I burst out laughing at that moment. I thought about the possibility that my son's pronunciation of *pa* might have sounded like *bap*.

However, my son's argument was very logical. How could a *bulgogi deopbap* not have any rice in it? Without any rice, it would just be *bulgogi*, not *deopbap*. As a chef, he should know the difference between these two menu items and should have confirmed the order with him if in doubt. In addition, he should not have gotten that angry and scolded him anyway even if his pronunciation were bad enough to be misunderstood.

The customer who witnessed the whole episode requested for a bowl of rice as a solution, saying that he could remove the green onions himself. So, the problem with the customer was solved, but the relationship between the chef and my son had deteriorated to the point of no return. From the restaurant owner's standpoint, there was no question that these two had to be separated, but since the chef was needed for cooking, it was my son who was transferred to a different job within the supermarket to end the dispute.

Truth be told, my younger son had attended a Korean language school when he was little and had been able to communicate well in Korean at the time. Then, when he became more interested in sports, he stopped going to the language school. Moreover, as he began spending more time speaking English with his older brother and friends and less speaking Korean with his grandparents while also learning more advanced vocabulary words from school, his Korean language ability naturally began declining. I regret now that I failed to keep him interested in and focused on studying Korean. I believe that my son has the same regrets now.

Language plays a crucial role in maintaining pride in one's identity and heritage. When we consider Korea's economic power and status in the international community these days, speaking fluent Korean could benefit one's career development. Fortunately, it is comforting to know that my younger son now recognizes the importance of learning Korean and has a desire to spend some time in Korea to study the language, culture, tradition, and its history.[25] It is late, but never too late.

25 As of 2021, he has not been able to carry out his desire to spend some time in Korea.

My Younger Son's Fingers

The Korea Times-Washington, D.C.
November 17, 2011

One Sunday evening, I was taking a short rest after going through the hectic weekend schedule. A phone call came from my younger son who was a junior in college. Out of the blue, he blurted out that he was just coming back from hospital and then burst into laughter.

He told me that he fractured a finger while paying basketball with his friends. It looked awful when he went to the hospital but was fine now after receiving a treatment. He assured me that everything was okay although he had to wait for a long time at the hospital. He hung up when his cab arrived to pick him up. Our conversation lasted less than a minute, but I was thankful that he had called me to share the news, and most of all, I was relieved that his voice was bright.

It was the third time that he injured his fingers. He had always loved playing basketball ever since he was little. Much like his parents, he did not have much in the way of height. However, he offset his vertical challenge with quickness and coordination. He had played for his high school team for all four years and had also been a team captain for three years, including his senior year. Thanks to him, I was able to enjoy watching many games. I always rooted for him with loud cheers and did not really care about what others would say about my cheering style—and sure enough, my son would often nag me about it.

My son was a point guard. He needed to run the team's offense, which required a lot of dribbling and creating scoring opportunities for the team. Therefore, his ball possession time had to be longer and the possibility of hand injuries was therefore much higher when compared to other players.

The first time he suffered a fractured finger was during a pre-season practice in his junior year of high school. He went to an orthopedic surgeon to receive a treatment and had to stop practicing for a few days. When the season began, he fastened the finger tightly with tapes and played with approval from the doctor.

He then fractured his finger again during a pre-season practice in his senior year. The situation then was a little different this time as it took a lot longer for his finger to heal. Also, the urgent care doctor who treated him did not readily authorize him to play. The doctor told my son that he could not play until the finger had fully healed. The coach, as he should, took the same position as the doctor. My son's frustration was growing when he had already missed two games. He felt the responsibility for the team as the starting point guard, and just sitting idly on the bench and watching the games he loved to play were unbearable.

Then my son made a surprising suggestion. He reasoned that as the emergency doctor was young, he might have lacked experience. That must be why he was being overly cautious. He wanted to go to the same orthopedic surgeon who treated his finger a year before and get a second opinion. That doctor might just allow him to play with his finger fastened tightly with tape just like the last time, especially now that some time had already passed since the injury. I thought that might just very well be possible, too. At the same time, I was worried that we would end up in a situation where we would have to decide which doctor to follow if there were conflicting diagnoses.

But my son was very firm—he could not wait for his finger to heal while sitting on the bench. He was willing to accept the consequences of aggravating the fracture if the other doctor allowed him to play. I could not ignore his request any longer and felt that he was now old enough to make his own decisions. We subsequently made an emergency appointment with the orthopedic surgeon, and my son's prediction was correct. The orthopedic surgeon gave him a permission to play with his fractured finger

Wooyoung at a basketball game

tightly taped up.

I can still see that the finger he had fractured back then is somewhat crooked today. I am not sure whether it is due to a natural after-effect of the injury or to his ignoring of the first doctor's advice. But nevertheless, he does not have any issue using the finger, and we, both he and I, do not have any regret about making the decision to play. In fact, I feel that it was the right judgment on my part to trust him and let him make his own decision. After all, it was the first time that he had made an important decision like that on his own. He had been so accustomed to asking his older brother for opinions and depending on him to help make decisions.

I still have this urge to intervene in his decision-making from time to time. Whenever that happens, I keep reminding myself not to interfere with him, and I pat myself on the shoulder for becoming a more mature father.

Girlfriend

The Korea Times–Washington, D.C.
August 24, 2010

My younger son was planning to go to the homecoming dance his freshman year in high school. A homecoming dance is normally held in the school cafeteria or the gym on the weekend of the homecoming football game.

As someone who immigrated to the U.S. in the middle of high school, I had never gone to a homecoming dance. I did not even go to senior prom, the graduation dance party, although Americans typically consider it to be one of the most memorable events of their high school days. My excuse at the time was that I did not have a partner to go with, but the truth was that I was simply not accustomed to the American culture of high school students going to dance parties.

My older son, who was three years older than the younger one, did not go to the homecoming dances either. However, the younger one insisted on attending the homecoming dance, most importantly, with a date. I gave him permission because there was no real good reason for me to block him from going. I also did not want to be accused of being narrow-minded and potentially face the criticism of how I could possibly serve on the school board without understanding the nature of important high school events like these—after all, I have never been to one myself! My younger son was not yet of the driving age, so it became my job to drive him and his date to dinner and then to the party. I also had to pick them up and drop off my son's date at her home after the party.

I soon found out that his date was a girl from our church and his girlfriend. I did not quite understand how she could become his girlfriend when they did not have much time to spend together at church. They were also attending different schools, so it would have been almost impossible for them to see each other regularly. Even so, I had to just accept the fact and hide my surprise. He was certainly much more advanced than I in dating girls. After all, I did not date anyone until after my junior year of college.

His girlfriend came to our house with her father. I took some pictures of the couple in front of the house and then drove them to the restaurant. I cannot remember what we talked about in the car, but I was thankful for the fact that a beautiful girl, wearing a pretty dress, liked my son.

When we arrived at the restaurant, my son took a deep breath as if he were getting ready for a battle. Come to think of it, he had never been to a restaurant either alone or bringing someone with him for whom he was responsible to take care of. Normally, he would just order his favorite food and I would be the one taking care of the bill for the family outings. He looked nervous now that he had to take care of everything on his own, ordering foods from the appetizers to the desserts and paying for the dinner, including tips. I almost burst out with laughter with a thought of watching him from a safe distance at my own table and also wanted to ask how he could date a girl when he was so anxious over a simple dinner. I forced myself to swallow the impulse.

The two of them did not have a chance to date outside of church even after that homecoming dance. Their relationship changed before the end of the year, and they decided to remain just as friends. Witnessing how their special relationship, seemingly started without any special motive, changed to a casual one again without any particular reason, I felt a generation gap. If it were for me, it would be awkward to face an ex-girlfriend after ending the relationship. It seems that kids of his age these days think differently than those from my generation. I could not tell whether the gap was simply generational or cultural.

I recently saw them again at church. They had both returned home from college for a break. They seemed to be happy to see each other again. They were even hugging! Huh, is this what younger generations are like!? It was a moment of reckoning that I lagged so far behind the younger generation. Instead of venturing into giving young people advice on dating, I should perhaps receive some professional training on the psychology of this new generation to understand them better. Otherwise, I would certainly be called a dinosaur for holding on to old-fashioned views on dating.

Singing The Star-Spangled Banner

April 2020

The first time I sang the American national anthem, "The Star-Spangled Banner", solo in public was in 2006. I was the chairman of the Fairfax County School Board at that time. The school system holds its annual leadership conference each year towards the end of the summer break. The attendees come from the approximately two hundred schools and school system's central offices, and more than fifteen hundred leaders of the school district attend every year. All the school board members are also invited. At the conference, the attendees review and discuss important issues in preparation for the upcoming new school year.

The national anthem is played at the opening ceremony of the conference and usually performed by a soloist. However, I was asked to sing at the 2006 conference. The request came from a person who knew that I was in our church choir. I gladly accepted the request as I was slated to give the opening greetings as the chairman of the school board anyway. Of course, there was piano accompaniment, and I was given an opportunity to rehearse a few times as well.

There were also some occasions in the past when I sang it unprepared. The most memorable one was at one of my younger son's basketball games. The game was held at one of the high schools in Arlington, Virginia. I had tried hard not to miss any of my son's basketball games no matter how busy I was. I was one of those loud parents who would cheer at the top of his lungs. Anyway, I was sitting in the stands and clearing my throat to get ready to cheer for the game. The players and the spectators were waiting for the national anthem to be played, but there seemed to be an issue with the machine that was supposed to play the pre-

Singing the National Anthem at the Leadership Conference

recorded national anthem—an announcement followed with a request for a volunteer to sing.

I had to make a split-second decision. Should I volunteer? It would be so embarrassing if I made a mistake, not only for me but for my son as well. The lyrics of the Star-Spanged Banner were not always easy to remember. The tune was even harder. If you did not get the first note at the right pitch, it would be all over—and there would be no accompaniment this time. If you started too high, it would be impossible to hit right notes for the part that went up even higher. On the other hand, starting too low would bring down the entire song. Perhaps my son could be proud of me if I managed to sing it well.

I debated what to do. There was not much time. I raised my hand and shouted that I would sing. Everyone looked at me. My son turned his head and gave me a surprised look. I could even hear the whispers coming from his teammates and the other parents seated in the stands. I rushed down to the center of the court and took the microphone. I announced my name at the request and further introduced myself as not only the father of a player but also a member of the Fairfax County School Board.

I then took a deep breath and there went the first pitch. It was perfect—now all I needed was to focus on the lyrics. No mistakes! I was so happy to hear the thunderous applause. My son looked pleased as well. That evening at home, he told me that he received numerous compliments from his teammates on my singing. He normally lectured me about my loud cheers after games, but this time, he did not complain about a thing. It was all good, and I felt great.

I was invited to sing the national anthem at my son's "senior night", the last home game for his entire high school basketball career. I had practiced several times in advance, but the first pitch came out about a half note lower than desired when I sang. I was somewhat disappointed but still thankful that I did not humiliate myself or my son by forgetting the lyrics.

I sometimes also had to sing the national anthem at school

board meetings when the singers did not show up without notice or we could not find any student available to sing during school vacations. I was also requested to sing at my last meeting as a member of the school board. At that meeting, a middle school orchestra was going to accompany me, but I found out that the pitch the orchestra would play was about a note below my preferred range. I asked whether the orchestra could bring play at one note higher but was told that it would be hard for the middle school students without more time to practice.

I was briefly conflicted whether to give up on singing it but finally decided to go ahead and sing it anyways since it was the last chance I would have to sing at a school board meeting. I thought it would be nice to have a "karaoke machine" that could easily adjust the accompaniment pitch. Anyway, now that I am retired from the school board, I do not know whether there will be another chance for me to sing "The Star-Spangled Banner" in public.

Chapter 3

Serving As A School Board Member

Introduction

I first read the news about the election for the Fairfax County School Board in 1993. There was an article in the Washington Post outlining how the members of the school board were going to be elected for the first time. I did not pay much attention at that time because the change would not come for another two years. I read a similar article again a year later, about a year prior to the election.

My involvement in politics prior to this moment was almost none. I occasionally acted as the master of ceremonies at some fundraising events for politicians seeking support from the local Korean American community. As many elderly Koreans were not fluent in English, I would act as a liaison and an interpreter. The second newspaper article about the school board election prompted me to think more seriously about running for the election. I reasoned that I might even have a chance, though not high, of winning, as it was for an education-related office. After all, Asians had always been generally recognized for placing great value in education.

When I was growing up in Korea, I thought that I had some leadership skills and found opportunities to build on them. I was the president of the student government in middle school, and public speaking was my forte. I had competed and won awards in numerous speech contests from seventh to tenth grade while in Korea. I may have subconsciously considered seeking an elected office someday.

However, I would not dare to think about running for election after immigrating to the U.S. My immediate priority was to adapt to the new immigrant life. I also thought it would be impossible for an Asian with a small stature and heavy accent to get votes from native-born Americans. Additionally, there had never previously been an Asian elected official in the area where I lived. Asian candidates had run on a few occasions, but never found success. Moreover, I did not know a thing about the electoral process.

Nevertheless, the newspaper article gave me an opportunity to look back at my life. My life in the U.S. until then was like living in America in words only and not necessarily much different from how I might be living if in Korea. I mostly associated Korean friends. I attended a Korean church, read Korean newspapers, and watched Korean videos. Almost all my clients at my law office were Koreans as well. I seldom spoke English.

Suddenly, I felt so humbled. I once had a big dream, but the immigrant life made me incapable to even think about it any longer. I needed to give myself a try. Winning or losing was not as important in fact, I did not expect to win. I also wanted to set an example for my own two sons born in the U.S. Most of all, I wanted to do it for myself. Just like that, I put all my effort into preparing for the election, and to everyone's surprise, including my own, I came out with a win in the election in November 1995, becoming the first Korean to be elected (to my knowledge) on the east coast of the U.S.

Although I failed to win in my re-election bid four years later, I did not give up. I patiently waited for another four years and another chance to run again. After a successful election, I was able to return to the school board. I also would end up challenging for an open position on the Fairfax County Board of Supervisors in a special election, where I lost by a mere difference of eighty-nine votes. That was painful. The Board of Supervisors is the governing body of the broad Fairfax County government, collaborating with the School Board on the work of Fairfax County Public Schools (FCPS).

The twenty years that I was able to serve as an elected school board member were truly precious moments in my life. It was a tremendous honor and opportunity to devote my youthful energy for so long to the education of students in the FCPS, one of the best school districts in the U.S. I continue to cheer on the staff and students for their amazing achievements.

Height

Washington Media
September 15, 1999

I am short. I cannot recall any time when I was not. I always sat in the front row of the class from first grade until I immigrated to the U.S. after my high school sophomore year. My attendance book numbers were always in the single digits in all those years except for one.[26]

I liked sitting in the front row because it was easier to read what was on the blackboard and was closer to the teachers. Obviously, this also meant that I could not doze off since it made me more visible to the teachers. I think that my lack of height came from my mother's side. My father was not short at all, but my mother was tiny. (I took after my father's side on stubbornness, though.) To further matters, my own two sons are far from being tall as well, just like their father.

However, being short was not an obstacle in my life. Of course, there were times when I had to really stretch to hold onto the handles above my head on public buses. I also could not dream of getting rebounds in basketball or spiking balls in volleyball matches; however, those impossibilities did not bother me since I had already given up on them from the start. My classmates did not tease me about my height—perhaps because I excelled academically.

---

26 When I was going to schools in Korea, the students in classrooms were seated in the order of their heights with the shortest students in the front row. The students' names on the attendance book also appeared in the order of the heights. The fact that my attendance book numbers were always in single digits meant that I had always been among the shortest nine students, with the class sizes ranging from about one hundred when I was in the first grade in elementary school to about sixty in high school.

It is weird that my height did not bother me much even in the U.S., although there were many more tall people here. I knew that there was no way for me to compete with the Americans in height, so I had no reason to worry about it. While living in Korea, I used to hear people talking about even a slight difference in height. The height differences among people in the U.S. are starker, yet people do not seem to talk about such differences as much. On average, Asians are shorter than Caucasians anyway.

Nevertheless, it would be a lie if I said that I had never felt uncomfortable with being short. In fact, there were times when I wished I were taller. On many occasions, I needed to greet women as a member of the school board and simple handshakes were not enough at times. I sometimes had to tiptoe to give a hug or a kiss to a taller woman and worried that I might have looked funny. Also, when a group picture was taken, my entire body would be covered by taller people if I stood in the back row; therefore, I would look around to find a relatively shorter person with whom I could stand. I also did not always enjoy being part of photo sessions at times if I were surrounded by all taller women.

Then one day I witnessed a student who confidently displayed that being short was nothing to be embarrassed about. I saw him last spring at the graduation ceremony of the Thomas Jefferson High School for Science and Technology, one of the best high schools in the U.S. I had been wanting to meet him for a long time, ever since I had heard that the senior class president of the school was a Korean. The graduation ceremony finally gave me a chance to meet him in person.[27] I was proud of the fact that the class president of such an excellent school was a Korean and I was

27 After graduating from high school, he studied at Princeton University. Later, he became a vice president at Allison Shearmur Productions in charge of production and distribution of movies, including the selection of movie scripts and directors and securing financing. The movies he participated in producing there included The Hunger Games, Cinderella, Rogue One: A Star Wars Story, and Dirty Dancing (2017 remake). In 2018, he moved onto Paramount Pictures. As of 2021, he is the Vice President of Production there.

pleased to hear his speech as well.

What made me happier, though, was that he was not much taller than I. He stood on the podium with the vice president, a girl. She seemed to be a head taller than he.[28] As they were taking turns to deliver a joint speech, using the same microphone fixed to the stand, I watched them with much curiosity to find out how they would handle the situation. Then, what I witnessed was beyond my imagination. The shorter class president brought out a step from under his chair and put it behind the podium to stand on. Not a single person laughed as if everyone were familiar with what he was doing. The entire process was also so smooth.

Being short is not a handicap. It is not something that one should be embarrassed about, either. Of course, it could cause some inconveniences but nothing that you could not overcome. It is just one of those discomforts that you might experience during a lifetime. I was inspired by how gracefully this young man handled his challenge. I should perhaps carry my own step to use when needed.[29]

---

28 The Korean student was on the crew and wrestling teams while the girl was on the basketball team.

29 The Korean student's parents read my column that appeared on Washington Media, and his father Mr. Dai H. Oh replied. His reply was published in the same paper. In it, he wrote, "Wouldn't it be nice if he were tall and could wear anything he wanted? Is that within his own control? Fortunately, God seems to be fair as my son has been given some other strengths in lieu of height. Unlike his parents who shy away from standing in front of other people, my son is active, has leadership skills, and gets along with other people very well, perhaps all due to his boy scout training...For our family, where my wife is a pharmacist, a step is a must-have for when we may not have the herbal medicine called uhwang-cheongsimhwan as a first aid medicine. (Uhwang-cheongsimhwan is a first aid medicine known for a quick cure for many illnesses.) Perhaps, we should get Mr. Moon a step as a gift." Since then, I have received large campaign donations from the student's father every time I ran for election.

The Korean student while standing on a step at his graduation

Cheek Kissing Practice

Washington Media
December 17, 1998

The first time I hugged a girl since puberty was during the summer after my high school junior year. To be honest, it was more that I was hugged as opposed to me doing the hugging.

As I had to repeat my high school sophomore year in the U.S. even though I had already completed it in Korea, I was the age of a college freshman by the summer after my high school junior year. I was given an opportunity to attend a Virginia Governor's School that summer. To my recollection, it was a four-week program, and I thoroughly enjoyed it. I stayed in a dormitory at Mary Baldwin College, a women's college located in the small city of Staunton. A group of students from this college acted as counselors for students participating in the program. I felt a little awkward living with American students for the first time in my life, but I managed to get along without problems for four weeks.

Finally, the program ended, and I packed my belongings to go back home. On my way to the Greyhound bus terminal, I met my student counselor. All that I remember after saying thanks to her was that I was in her arms. It was the first time that I was hugged by a woman! My heart started pounding, maybe because she was about the same age as I. I am sure that it was only a moment, but it certainly felt forever to me at the time. I finally said a goodbye after the long hug. The warmth from the hug remained in my heart and did not disappear until I reached the bus terminal.

One of the more uncomfortable moments that I have had to bear as a member of the school board was learning how to greet women. I still have not fully learned how to greet women, even after experiencing that sudden hug while in high school. It is relatively easier when it is a first encounter as a verbal greeting is generally sufficient. However, it is different when I meet an acquaintance whom I have not seen for a long time. Of course, I can give a light kiss on the cheek or a hug with my arms lightly around the shoulder. Yet it is easier said than done as my body would often become stiff.

At a school board meeting a few months ago, I met a woman with whom I had previously served together on the school board for several years. I had even known her prior to our time on the board, and she had always been kind to me—so I was so happy to see her again. I decided to give her a light kiss on the cheek, but somehow a loud kissing sound was emitted that, I was sure, could have been heard from afar. She looked somewhat awkward, or at least that was what I thought. I pretended to be cool. In truth, I felt so embarrassed and hoped to find a rat hole in which to hide.

There was another episode a few weeks ago. I attended a PTA meeting in my district where I met a lady who had supported me greatly in the past. The nightmare of embarrassing myself with a loud kissing sound flashed through my mind, so I just greeted her verbally and turned around. That was when I noticed that she was sticking out her cheek and waiting for a customary kiss. Certainly, another uncomfortable moment, but I could not turn back around and just walked away. I still cannot shake off that embarrassing episode from my memory.

It has been almost twenty-five years since I started a new life in the U.S. I attended schools here in the U.S. from high school to law school. I have worked as a lawyer for the past fourteen years and more than three years as a member of the school board. However, it seems that I still have not fully adapted to American culture. It proves the point that it is not that easy to acclimate to a culture that is not your own.

I should perhaps practice more in kissing women's cheeks in the forthcoming year.

A Word Of Encouragement

The Korea Times–Washington, D.C.
June 1, 2018

I visited an elementary school last week to meet someone who would be starting her job as the new principal of the school in July. The visit was initially planned to take place a few weeks earlier when the announcement of the new principal was made, but I missed it because it was somehow not recorded on my calendar. Thus, I decided to visit her last week to congratulate and apologize to her at the same time.

There are about 200 public schools in Fairfax County and several dozen schools get new principals each year. I do not always attend every announcement of a new principal; however, remembering how I have always emphasized the importance of appointing principals with an Asian background, the regional assistant superintendents would send me notifications of the public announcement whenever an Asian principal was selected so that I could attend the announcement at the school, if possible.

The new principal of the school that I visited last week was Asian. As usual, a regional assistant superintendent had notified me about the announcement in advance, and I had happily promised to attend. Then, I missed it and felt bad for the many people, including the new principal, who might have expected my visit. For that reason, I felt the need to visit this school.

No less important was the fact that the new principal was Korean. Up until that point, there was only one other principal among all elementary school principals who was of Korean descent as she had a Korean mother. There had previously been one middle school principal of Korean descent, but he moved into a new role and currently works in the central office of the school system.

With the newly appointed Korean principal

There is another middle school principal with a Korean mother;[30] but, for high schools, there has yet to be any principal of Korean origin.

This new Korean principal is young and has not reached forty yet. Of course, there have been cases of even younger principals. Even so, she became a principal at a young age, quite unthinkable if she were in Korea. It also meant that she possessed outstanding qualities. When I finally met and congratulated her on her new position, I also had a chance to talk about her family.

During our conversation, she told me that her parents knew me well. She also reminded me that I had treated her with a breakfast not long after she first had become a teacher. I asked her father's name out of curiosity and then remembered it instantly when I heard his name. Indeed, I remembered having had breakfast with her at her father's request a long time ago. Her father asked me to give her some words of encouragement as she embarked upon the career of an educator.

Honestly, I could not remember what we had talked about over that breakfast. According to her, however, I had advised her to consider becoming a principal. That was not anything that she had on her mind at the time as she had only just started teaching. Nevertheless, she took my words to her heart and finally became a principal.

I was quite pleased to hear that she followed my advice. To tell the truth, I did not know whether she, a young teacher, had the qualities to become a principal when I first met her. I might have said it out of courtesy, but she had kept it in her heart. It made me realize all over again the importance of our words as they could affect a person for a long time, whether in a good or bad way. This is also part of the reason why I, as a member of the school board, must always think deeply and carefully before giving advice.

I asked her a question during our conversation last week. "Are you currently pursuing a doctoral degree?" I added that a doctoral

---

30 She subsequently became a high school principal in 2020.

degree would be beneficial if she wanted to advance further in her career. She shook her head and responded that she was quite content with her current position as a principal. I advised her to have a plan in place even if for a long term of five to ten years, as no one knew what the future would hold. Of course, it would be important for her to discuss it with her family as she currently was raising young children.

I hoped that she would again keep my words of advice for a long time and that my words might become a seed for more good things to happen in her life. In addition, I added a request that she would now continue taking on the role of giving out advice to the younger teachers. Regardless of what others might say, she had already become a role model for young teachers to follow.

Bob Frye, Former School Board Member

The Korea Times-Washington, D.C.
October 20, 2010
December 11, 2015

I attended a worship service last Sunday afternoon at the Virginia Theological Seminary, an Anglican seminary located in Alexandria, Virginia. The Dean's Cross Award was presented during the service.

One of the three award recipients this year was Mr. Robert E. Frye, a former colleague of mine on the Fairfax County School Board. Founded in 1823, the seminary has been providing theological education based on Anglican theology at a graduate school level for almost two hundred years. The seminary is familiar to me as it is located not far from where I used to live when I first arrived in the U.S., and I often passed by it.

The Dean's Cross Award was established in 2008. Each year, the dean of the seminary, in consultation with the chairman of the seminary's board of trustees, recognizes leaders who carry out their baptismal vows to pursue world peace and justice and respect the dignity of all people.

Each recipient is given not just an award certificate but also a handmade silver cross that is a replica of the cross at the seminary chapel. Barbara Bush, a former first lady, was one of the other recipients of the award this year. For Mrs. Bush, the award was delivered to her on Mother's Day at a church in Houston, Texas, as she could not attend the ceremony in Alexandria, Virginia, in person.

Mr. Bob Frye had served as a member of the Fairfax County

School Board for nineteen years, eleven years as an appointed member and eight years as an elected member. He and I were among those who were elected in the first school board election in Fairfax County in November 1995. He had served two four-year terms as an elected member before retiring from the board at the end of 2003. He had also worked for the federal government for many years before retiring in 1999. He turned seventy-nine this year.

With the former School Board member Mr. Robert Frye
at a political event (2019)

Mr. Frye and I have a special relationship. The first agenda item of the first elected school board in January 1996 was to elect the board's chairman. The eight Democrats out of the twelve total board members decided to meet before the start of the term to discuss whom to support for chairman. There were two candidates vying for the position. One of them was Ms. Amundson, a white woman already on the board at the time, and the other was Mr. Frye, an African American man. Each of them was given a chance to make a pitch for candidacy, and then the two were excused. After they left the meeting, the remaining six Democrats deliberated on the selection and eventually decided to support the Ms. Amundson to be the chairman.

Shortly thereafter I received a phone call from Mr. Frye who heard about our selection. He told me that he had not thought that the six members would have come up with the decision so quickly and that he was not willing to accept the decision. He then asked me why I did not support him. I answered that it was more accurate to say that I supported the other candidate more rather than not supporting him. I further said that, if he wanted my support, he would have to prove his chairmanship quality to me. I added that I had witnessed the leadership quality of Ms. Amundson during the immediate six months that I had worked with her together on the board. What I meant to convey to him was that I had not had an opportunity yet to learn about his leadership qualities.

However, Mr. Frye's reaction to me at that point was something for which I was not prepared. Mr. Frye claimed that African American leaders always had to prove their qualities again even when they were already known to have those qualities. I was taken aback by his reaction. What I had said to him did not stem from any prejudice on my part toward African Americans. Never had I realized that what I had said could be taken that way and hurtful to him, even though it was true that I spoke without thinking deeply about the painful history of African Americans in this country. That incident became a lifetime lesson for me to think before speaking out.

Mr. Frye ran for the chairmanship against Ms. Amundson anyway and the result was not favorable to him. He only received two votes out of the eight Democratic members, one from another African American member and one from himself. The rest of the Democrats, including myself, all voted for Ms. Amundson. However, the four Republican members supported Mr. Frye, resulting in a six-to-six tie. After a few more rounds of deadlock, the African American member who had initially voted for Mr. Frye finally decided to honor our previous agreement and changed her vote to elect Ms. Amundson as the chairman.

After Ms. Amundson had served as the chairman for two one-year terms, there came another chairman's election in January 1998. At that time, the candidates were Mr. Frye and Dr. Emery, a white male who had served as the vice chairman for the past two years. Dr. Emery also expressed his desire to serve for two terms as the chairman. The election for chairman was headed for another six-to-six tie again.

I volunteered to be an arbiter and urged both Mr. Frye and Dr. Emery to take turns with each serving for one term only as the chairman. For example, Dr. Emery would first serve as the chairman while Mr. Frye serving as the vice chairman for one year and then Mr. Frye would take on the chairman's position in the following year. I also firmly added that neither of them would get my support unless they agreed to my suggestion. At the end, a gentleman's agreement was reached, and Mr. Frye was later elected as the chairman a year after Dr. Emery's chairmanship for one term first. As such, Mr. Frye became the first African American to serve as the chairman of the school board in the history of Fairfax County.

As I was about to walk into the Emmanuel Chapel last Sunday, a somewhat familiar looking woman came towards me and greeted me. She told me that she had heard the story of how Mr. Frye had become the chairman of the school board. That was something that I honestly had almost forgotten about. My intervention must have been worthwhile after all. I gave myself a pat on the back.

Attending Orientation For New Teachers

The Korea Times–Washington, D.C.
August 26, 2015

I attended the opening ceremony of the orientation for new teachers to Fairfax County Public Schools last Monday. The weeklong orientation for new teachers is held every August. As usual, the Apple Federal Credit Union Education Foundation provided enough grant money to cover most of the funding needed for the orientation. Approximately twelve hundred out of the two thousand newly hired teachers attended it. This countywide orientation is open to all new teachers, but participation itself is voluntary.

I have attended the opening ceremony almost every year and even gave a keynote speech last year. The most important reason for my attending the ceremony is to show the new teachers that there is a minority, especially one of Asian origin, on the school board. Only two out of twelve board members attended the ceremony this year, and I was one of the two—last year, I happened to be the only one.

To begin the ceremony, the board members were first introduced, followed by senior officials of the central administrative office. I felt something unusual again this year when the regional assistant superintendents were introduced. There are currently five regions within the school district in Fairfax County—they used to be called "areas". There were four "areas" when I first began my school board tenure, which was reduced to three at one point to reduce costs and to improve administrative efficiencies. Subsequently, the number increased all the way to eight, and the "area" was renamed to become the "cluster". Eventually, they then became the current five "regions" we know today after yet another reorganization based on the recommendation from the current superintendent, who had been newly appointed at the time.

The regional assistant superintendents direct and supervise about forty schools each within their respective regions. They evaluate the performance of the principals and handle constituent matters unresolved at the principal level. They also play a vital role in the selection of the new principal when a vacancy occurs. Of course, the final decision on selection of a new principal is made by the superintendent based on the evaluations from an interview panel and with consent of the school board.

However, a recommendation from the regional assistant superintendent is really the key in the final decision-making. As we all know, principals have the full authority and responsibility for hiring all faculty and staff of their schools as well as for interacting with parents. Therefore, the position of a regional assistant superintendent is vested with great authority—demonstrating responsibility is critical.

All five regional assistant superintendents are currently minorities[31]—four are African Americans, with the other being a Latin American who immigrated to the U.S. when he was in his 20s. However, the superintendent and the other assistant superintendents who oversee human resources, finance, facilities, special and general educations, information technology, and communications are all white.[32] In other words, the top leaders responsible for administration and technical support from the

---

31 As of October 2021, there are two black, two white, and one Hispanic Regional Assistant Superintendents, and the assistant superintendent in charge of special education is also a black

32 As of October 2021, the Deputy Superintendent, Chief Operating Officer, and Chief Equity Officer are all black. The previous Chief Operating Officer was a Korean woman.

central offices for the educational bureaucrats are white, and those responsible for public relations where they need to interact with the public and directly supervise schools are African American.

I have learned that elementary and secondary school educators are highly respected within the African American community; many, particularly smart female students, choose teaching as their career. Thus, it is not surprising that the two of the four African American regional assistant superintendents are women.

According to a recent report, ten percent of Fairfax County residents are African Americans, and the percentage of African American teachers is just over eight percent. However, a point noteworthy to make is that more than sixteen percent of those teachers currently participating in the special career development program are African American.

On the other hand, Asians fall significantly behind them. While Asians make up about nineteen percent of the total county population, Asian teachers represent less than six percent so far. Furthermore, Asian teachers make up barely three percent of the participants in the special career development program. There is a long way to go for Asians in K-12 public school teaching. I pray for more young Asians to step up and to have a dream in public school teaching.

A Story From Visit To Korea With The Superintendent

The Korea Times-Washington, D.C.
December 5, 2014

I would like to share a story from the visit to Korea in late October with Dr. Karen Garza, Superintendent of the Fairfax County Public Schools, and her sister, along with Tim Thomas, the principal of Westfield High School.

Dr. Garza had lived in Texas all her life until her appointment as Superintendent in Fairfax County last year. Born in Texas, she attended elementary to high schools and then college and graduate school as well, all in Texas. She had continued to live in Texas throughout her career as a teacher and had served as a superintendent there as well. As she had spent her entire life in Texas, I was concerned about how she would find the food in Korea.

The first time she had Korean food was in Fairfax County last May. As the chairman of the school board at that time, I had arranged my first meeting with her over a meal before she would officially take the position of superintendent on July 1. I chose a Korean restaurant because I felt that she needed to get used to foods from different cultures represented in multi-racial and multi-cultural Fairfax County. Of course, I selected a restaurant offering a buffet so that she could have more selections.

Before the visit to Korea, I had received inquiries from several people in Korea who would be hosting us about the food preferences of the superintendent. My response had been consistent that they should not worry about it as she should explore and learn about the traditional Korean foods anyway. Thus, she was able to experience many different Korean dishes even though we tried to avoid the foods with distinctively strong flavors. However, we learned that there was a limit to it.

We went to Busan, a large port city located in the southeastern corner of the country. We could not miss seeing the beach, so we went to Gwanganri Beach after checking in at the hotel. Later, we went to a seafood restaurant for dinner at the recommendation of a cab driver. I knew that Dr. Garza did not eat sashimi, but I still thought that it would be good for her to experience what the sashimi platter looked like. Plus, there would be other seafood like grilled fish for her to eat anyway.

The first dish that came out was full of live octopus and the amount was substantial for all five of us there. When she saw the live octopus wriggling, Dr. Garza immediately turned her face from it. It seemed that she also lost her appetite right at that moment as she could not even touch the grilled fish that followed. Therefore, it was just one Korean education consultant, acting as our guide at the time, and myself who received the windfall of enjoying the entire five servings of live octopus to ourselves. Meanwhile, Mr. Tim Thomas, a white male principal, courageously took a bite, which granted him bragging rights to claim to have eaten live octopus.

When we finally came out of the restaurant, I spotted a street vendor selling steamed silkworm pupae in front of the restaurant. I decided to take things a step further since I figured the American guests had already seen live octopus now, so I bought a cup of pupae. Everyone looked at pupae with curiosity and listened to my explanation of what they were. Then, when they saw me eating them, they looked at me as if they were witnessing a savage.

I explained to them that pupae were a healthy delicacy which I enjoyed very much when I was young, but I could only afford to buy after saving up my allowances. None of them wanted to try it, though, no matter how I cajoled them. Afterwards we began walking along the beach, but the superintendent and her sister wanted to excuse themselves to go back to the hotel early. I was told the next day that they had ordered a pizza and a bottle of wine from their hotel room.

Superintendent Dr. Karen Garza and her younger sister
at a seafood restaurant in Busan, Korea

When we were visiting Tongyeong, South Gyeongsang Province, we were invited to a dinner at an Italian restaurant inside the Yun Isang Music Hall. It was too bad that I could not have sashimi in Tongyeong, but I decided to compromise. Nevertheless, even at that restaurant, we were able to experience the differences in food culture. All the foods served there were bland in comparison to Italian dishes in the U.S. While many salty Korean foods do exist, American foods generally contain higher level of sodium. That is perhaps why there are so many Americans suffer from high blood pressure.

Anyhow, the superintendent and the principal must have told the live-octopus story to others after returning to Fairfax County. I heard from many people that they had seen the video of the live octopus taken at the restaurant in Korea. Of course, they did not leave out the story of how much I seemed to have enjoyed eating them. I have a suspicion that the video might be included in the orientation materials for anyone who would travel to Korea with me in the future.

Seating Etiquette

The Korea Times-Washington, D.C.
November 29, 2019

I recently returned from a visit to Korea. A regional assistant superintendent and a principal from the Fairfax County Public Schools, where I am currently serving as a member of the school board, joined me on this ten-day trip. For the past several years, I have been visiting Korea with American educators each year instead of taking vacation.

Sometimes, it is hard to guide the American educators on their first trip to Korea, but I have felt that the benefits for our educators to learn from diverse cultures and education systems can never be overstated. For that reason, I have gladly volunteered my time and efforts to introduce my home country. As there are many Korean students in Fairfax County, these trips will also help educators have better understanding of the Korean students and their parents.

We visited many places in Korea on this trip as usual. We started from Seoul and then went to Incheon, Yeosu, Daegu, Busan, Geoje, and Gyeongju. These are the four largest cities in the country, two southern cities famous for their archipelagos, and the country's most historical city. We visited schools and met with Korean educators and students. Our Fairfax County educators also had the opportunity to learn some unique Korean etiquettes as well, including one about seating.

We were usually invited to the principals' offices when we visited schools in Korea. The principals' offices invariably displayed a table and chairs not easily found in the schools in the U.S. While there were some differences between the schools, the tables could be described generally as being low to the ground, either round or rectangular in shape, and the equally low chairs were always placed around the tables. Regardless of the shape of the tables, it was easy to identify the head seats. Of course, it was cvcn morc obvious when the table was rectangular. The head seats were normally reserved for the principals.

One day, we visited a school in Incheon and the regional assistant superintendent of where the school was located joined us. We were guided to the principal's office and the principal asked the regional assistant superintendent to take the head seat. The regional assistant superintendent, however, declined it several times saying that it was not her seat. However, that did not mean that the principal could sit in that chair, either. It would be out of place for a principal to sit in the head chair when his superior, the assistant superintendent, was present. The assistant superintendent was not sitting in that chair out of courtesy to me who was visiting the school as a member of the school board from another country. I could not take the head seat, either, as I was there only as a guest.

Visiting Bitgaram Elementary School in South Jeolla Province, Korea (November 1, 2018)

Anyway, people started sitting down around the table, leaving the head seat empty but one chair short. The principal brought in a chair from another room and sat in it. The head seat was still left empty. Witnessing the whole incident, the American educators were deeply touched by Korean's consideration for and humility towards their seniors.

We encountered another comparable situation while visiting a school in Daegu. The deputy superintendent of the Daegu Metropolitan City accompanied us. We were sitting around a table and the deputy superintendent sat in the head seat just because the principal could not sit in it. The deputy superintendent was a long-time acquaintance of mine, and he appeared to be uncomfortable with the arrangement. When one person had to leave early while the meeting was still in progress, the deputy superintendent quickly moved to the seat of the departing person as soon as it became empty.

His gesture was quite refreshing to the American educators. The deputy superintendent, the highest ranked person amongst the Korean educators attending the meeting, must have felt that sitting in the head seat in presence of a member of the school board from another country was inappropriate. It was done in respect for me, and his action took the American educators by surprise.

I do not mean to imply that that the Korean culture of seating etiquette is superior or that American educators should necessarily emulate this etiquette. However, experiencing this unique culture would be beneficial for them and in the education of the students under their care, especially considering the high diversity and the multi-cultural backgrounds of Fairfax County students and families. Hopefully, our American educators would consider extending the same etiquette when interacting with the Koreans in the U.S.

At Panmunjom (2017)[33]

33 The person standing next to me was the Deputy Superintendent and the two white men in the back were high school principals at the time. Subsequently, the Deputy Superintendent became the superintendent in a school district in Maryland and one of the principals was promoted to an executive principal position. The American educators were at first cautious with the visit to Panmunjom but expressed their appreciation for the opportunity after the visit. They felt that it was an invaluable experience. I could see them becoming tense as they saw the barbed wires along the side of the highway leading to Panmunjom.

Football Awards Ceremony

The Korea Times-Washington, D.C.
March 10, 2017

With an award recipient at the ceremony (2019)

I was quite busy last weekend, from Friday night to Sunday night. I attend many community events as a member of the school board, but I cannot say that it is always with full enthusiasm. For some events, I have no choice, and for some others, I go with some reluctance as I cannot say no to the invitations. Every so often, I personally find it hard to attend a particular event but do it anyway out of sense of a mission, and the event on the last Sunday afternoon fell into that category.

The event was hosted by the Northern Virginia Football Hall of Fame. The host organization evaluates, recognizes, and gives awards for the achievements, efforts, and contributions made by prominent players, coaches, volunteers, cheerleaders, and referees in the youth football at this annual event. Selections of the best players from the neighborhood and high school leagues and new inductees to the Hall of Fame are officially announced at the event. There were two inductees this year, a person who had overseen the sports and recreation programs in the City of Alexandria for a long time and a former professional football player from the Dallas Cowboys who had graduated from Osbourn High School.[34]

The event this year was in its twenty-seventh year, and I had been attending this event for many years myself. I always need to remind myself when attending that the event could be quite lengthy. It includes a dinner starting at around 3:30 p.m. There is even a reception prior to the event for about an hour. The actual awards do not begin until after the dinner and easily last for another three hours. By the time the entire program ends, it is almost 8 p.m., so almost five hours in total for the event.

However, it is surprising to see that a large majority of the attendees stay until the very end of the program despite its length. Everyone must have been well trained for endurance through the football practices. Other elected officials from the local areas including congressmen also often attend this event; however, many of them leave soon after they are introduced or their parts of participation in giving out awards are done. Of course, the attendees understand that elected officials generally maintain busy schedule even on weekends, but I had always found it difficult to leave early and most of the time stayed until the end. This past

34 Based in Manassas, Virginia.

Sunday's event was no exception.

The reason that I had not been able to leave early is due to my self-consciousness of being not only a school board member but also almost always one of the very few Asians present at the event itself. Even in my twenty-second year of public service, I am still very conscious about my racial background. It is still not common to see an Asian elected official at mainstream social events, especially at events like the one held last Sunday. Asian students and their parents do not necessarily stand out in sports like football; thus, it is difficult to catch a glimpse of Asians amongst the volunteers, coaches, referees, or the players receiving awards in football. Almost all the attendees at this type of event are white or African American.

Almost six hundred people packed the hotel ballroom attending the event last Sunday. I would guess that the Asian presence seemed less than one percent, and even the youngest students were staying in place until the end of the events. So instead of leaving early, I looked for more opportunities to participate in the presentation of awards to become more visible. I wanted to show that there was an Asian among the crowd of mostly white and African American attendees. I sometimes ask myself whether I am being narrow-minded, but I will continue doing what I have been doing thus far until I can answer that question with confidence. I wish for the day to come soon for all sports and other activities to show much more even participation among students from different ethnic backgrounds.

A Proud Father

Washington Media
January 13, 1999

It was about a year ago when I met Mr. Joe Gartlan, a state senator of Virginia, at the reception hosted by the Fairfax Education Association. Mr. Gartlan represents the Mason Neck area near Mount Vernon. I had previously met him a few times at public events, but it was at this reception where I was able to have a long talk with him for the first time.

Mr. Gartlan is seventy-two years old. A former lawyer, he has served as a member of the Virginia State Senate for the past thirty years. He said that he was grateful for the opportunity to serve in public office for so many years although it had not been always easy.

I was envious and surprised that he had been able to serve continuously for so long, so I asked him where his motivation had come from. His answer to me then was totally unexpected. "Money, Power, and Greed," he said. He explained that it was the same response that he had provided to a voter a long time ago. He further commented that the response was a half-joke but was enough to silence the voter.

I must face another election this November myself. The voters will judge my performance and achievements for the first time since being elected in November 1995 for a four-year term. Campaigning in the first election in 1995 was hard. I did not know anything about running for election. This time, despite having a little bit more knowledge and experience, I am now even more nervous than before, and it is not fun to think about the hard work that I need to put in again.

Reflecting upon Senator Gartlan's reasons for staying in the office for thirty years, I asked myself why I wanted to run again. "Money?" I am certain that it is not for the money. Of course, I am not going to claim that the annual salary of eight thousand dollars does not help at all.[35] The net take-home income after taxes pays for a car. However, the pay is still too little when the amount of time that I need to stay away from my law practice and my family is considered.

Then, is it "Power?" I cannot quite say "no" to that with conviction. Power is like a drug that once you taste it, you cannot let it go, and the position of a school board member seems to provide its own taste of it. Of course, I try to enjoy the taste in a positive way as much as possible. I often handle constituent complaints by calling the principals or the central administrative offices of the school system; however, the true power of the school board members come from the decision-making authority on the budget, personnel, and the education policy, especially being responsible for an annual budget of more than 1.2 billion dollars and twenty thousand employees.[36]

"Greed?" It would be lying to myself if I denied it. To tell the truth, I am greedy. I am so for work and for desire for recognition, praise, and respect by others. I am greedy for honor and fame and want to become a role model for other people. I also want to be

35 The annual salary for the school board members has increased a few times since then and is now thirty-two thousand dollars. However, with the median household income in Fairfax County being over one hundred twenty thousand dollars, it is not a large amount. When the amount of time needed to be devoted is considered, it is even more so. The work of a school board member is not a job and does not necessitate a fulltime position. However, over my time in office, I have been spending about thirty hours a week. A salary increase can only be made by the school board during the first six months of the election year. If the salary is increased, the voters will render their judgment on it in the election to be held in November of the same year.

36 As of 2020, the annual budget is 3.2 billion dollars, and the number of employees is twenty-five thousand fulltime equivalents.

seen as always doing my best in everything that I do. The most precious greed of all is my desire to be remembered as the proud father by my own two sons.

I would like to win again in the election this fall. The salary may be small, but I would like to put into good use the power that would come with the position of a school board member. I want to use it in fair and valuable ways and for the benefit of our future generation. I do not think that my sons will lose respect for me even if I lose. However, I would still like to win and demonstrate to my sons how I tried my best in all circumstances.

Lessons Learned From Election Losses

The Korea Times-Washington, D.C.
July 20, 2011

I have run in six elections so far, winning four but also losing two.[37] The first election was for the Fairfax County School Board in 1995. At that time, I ran for the Braddock District seat and did not expect to win.

I did not know enough about the education issues at the time. Nor did I have any experience with campaigning in an election. My activities outside the Korean community were minimal, and my name recognition was close to zero. My campaign manager did not expect me to win, either. My personal goal was to show everyone that I, at least, did my best in campaigning. However, to everyone's surprise, I ended up winning by outperforming the two opponents. I received fifty-one percent of the votes, defying everyone's predictions.

A bitter taste of a loss came in the re-election campaign four years later in 1999. Unlike the first time, everyone was certain that there was no way that I would lose in the re-election. Local pundits counted on my incumbency, the knowledge and the skills gained during the past four years, prior campaigning experience, and the higher name recognition for an easy win this time. Unfortunately, the pundits were wrong again. I lost to the same Republican candidate that I had defeated by fourteen points in the first election.

Come to think of it, however, it was inevitable that I would lose that election. You must always do your best regardless of the

37 Including my wins in the subsequent elections in 2011 and 2015, I have now won five times and lost twice.

circumstances to win, but I did not. Campaigning for the re-election in 1999, I tried to avoid much of the same hard work that I had previously encountered four years earlier. Door-knocking on the voters' houses is the best way to secure votes, but that is also the hardest work. In the first election, I was not always welcome by the voters I visited. There were some nasty people. At times, people would just slam their doors in my face. It was terrifying to think about having to face such people again. Therefore, using the legal work that I would need to do for clients and the potential health hazard of dangerously sweltering summer temperatures as excuses, I tried to avoid knocking on doors as much as possible—and the result was brutally honest. Fortunately, I was unwilling to give up.

Watching the election returns (2003)

Undeterred by the loss in the re-election, I ran again four years later in 2003, this time for a countywide at-large seat on the school board and won, thus becoming a comeback kid. I ran for the re-election of my at-large seat in 2007 and won again for my third four-year term.[38] The painful failure in 1999 was a blessing in disguise.

Nevertheless, I experienced another heartbreaking loss in 2009. Sharon Bulova, the Braddock District Supervisor of the Fairfax County Board of Supervisors, had become the chairman of the Board of Supervisors. A special election was held to elect her successor for the Braddock District seat.[39] I ran and prevailed by a big margin in the Democratic primary after tough campaigning. Intra-party competition can be more draining on you as you often run against a friend in the same political party.

On the Republican side, however, there was only a single candidate and, therefore, there was no need for a primary to choose the party's candidate. The Republican candidate was able to just campaign without wasting resources and waited for the Democratic primary winner to emerge.

By the time I had become the Democratic nominee by winning in the primary, the Braddock District Democratic Committee became split into two groups—one supporting me and another supporting my primary opponent. The supporters of my primary opponent who believed in their candidate and expected her to win were deeply hurt.

---

38 There are nine district and three at-large school board members in Fairfax County.

39 The supervisors are the ultimate decision-makers in the county government and decide the county's share of the public education budget. As of 2019, the county's share is more than seventy percent of the entire budget for the school system in Fairfax County. Reliance on the local funding support is high in Fairfax County. In the U.S. where local autonomy is well established, there are various structures of the county government. As for Fairfax County, the Board of Supervisors holds both executive and legislative decision-making authorities.

With only four weeks left until the special election, I was not able to heal their hurts and bring them over to help my campaign. I was left with no choice but to campaign without their support. I was overwhelmed in facing the Republican opponent and his party's support, united in solidarity from the beginning. I lost the election by a mere margin of eighty-nine votes.

Looking back, I should have reached out to the losing primary opponent more aggressively. In fact, I met with her in person and formally requested for her help; however, when her reaction was lukewarm, I did not pursue any further, which I should have done. As the primary winner, I should have displayed more humility and sought her support more earnestly. It was incumbent upon me to play the leading role to put an end to the emotional bitterness between the two camps, but I had failed. I had not done my job.

In preparation for another school board election in November this year, I am reflecting upon the lessons that I learned from my previous failures. Most importantly, I should not take this re-election for granted. I cannot afford to be lazy. Furthermore, as a senior colleague among the Democratic candidates running for the countywide at-large seats, I need to assume the role of a leader with a mindset to help them out throughout the campaign season. My supporters do not expect any less from me, and that is how I should pay back my debt to them.

A campaign kick-off (2011)

Chapter 4

American Education Stories

My second son's best high school friends[40]

My younger son was pretty stressed out when applying for college. I had graduated from Harvard, and his older brother

40 Both of his friends are tall. The friend on the left is six feet three inches and the one on the right, six feet eight inches. It is quite a scene to watch the three of them walking together with my son in the middle.

was an undergraduate student there at the time. His mother had graduated from Seoul National University, the top college in Korea. He and his two best friends from Thomas Jefferson High School for Science and Technology made a pledge and set a goal to attend Harvard together. However, my younger son was not admitted to Harvard—he was placed on the waiting list, whereas his two best friends were both accepted to Harvard.

He did receive an offer, however, from Brown, another Ivy league college. Still, he was devastated because he had been longing to go to Harvard for so long. Both of his parents were feeling the same disappointment. We as parents knew that we should console him, but it was difficult to stay calm. It seemed that my first son was more mature than anyone else in the family. He argued that it was not necessary for anyone to go to Harvard. Brown was an excellent school, he emphasized, and his brother would receive as good an education there as at Harvard.

Watching my younger son struggling, I sought advice from one of my fellow Harvard graduates. She was an alumna volunteer and had served for a long time as the president of the local Harvard Schools Committee helping the admissions office with interviewing and screening applicants. She was four years my senior, and I hoped to learn from her what I could do to help my son get off the waiting list. She then shared with me a story about her youngest son.

She had three sons. Her husband and her first two sons also went to Harvard. Her youngest son was also accepted to Harvard; however, he decided to go to Brown instead after visiting the schools and carefully reviewing the programs each college was offering. Everyone in her family respected his decision. No one raised any objection. She added that Brown was a fine school and that I should not get too obsessed with Harvard.

The roommate that my younger son had during his freshman year at Brown was Caucasian and a lacrosse player. He had been accepted to Harvard but chose Brown—he felt more comfortable with Brown and did not want to go to Harvard just for its name's sake. My younger son eventually came to love Brown, excelled academically there, and met many good friends. He became actively engaged in extracurricular activities as well. He majored in physics and received a thesis award at the graduation ceremony, an award only given to two graduates among the physics majors that year.

At my second son's graduation from Brown University (2013)

Sky Castle

The Korea Times-Washington, D.C.
February 8, 2019

I recently watched the entire twenty episodes of Sky Castle, a TV drama that was the hottest topic of discussion in Korea. The drama was about the fierce competition for college admissions in Korea. I watched the first half through short YouTube video clips available online, so I might have missed some content here and there. For the second half, I searched for the full versions and watched them in a week. I missed a lot of sleep at night.

I first became interested in this drama because the admissions coordinator appearing in the drama was introduced as someone coming from my very own Fairfax County. I was curious about how Fairfax County was portrayed in the drama. I met two educators visiting Fairfax County from Korea about ten days ago, and they told me that Fairfax County had now become even more famous in Korea with this drama. That added to my curiosity. As the drama dealt with many educational issues, especially the college admissions considered to be so important by students and parents alike, it naturally attracted my attention.

However, I was not happy with the story line in the drama as it related to Fairfax. In the story, the coordinator from Fairfax was described as being someone obsessed with her daughter's success, mainly out of her jealousy towards a former college classmate of hers in Korea. This obsession led to the murder of her husband, which was then disguised as an accident. Her only daughter became handicapped because of that accident.

The story also described her assistant as a former drug addict who used to wander around the streets of Fairfax at night. As I heard that the drama was about the overheated preparation process for the college admissions, I had initially assumed that it might portray something similar happening in Fairfax—fortunately, that was not the case.

Nevertheless, I felt that the drama was worth watching for all Korean parents, not just in Fairfax, but across the whole U.S. The stories in the drama are all fiction and offer dramatizations of real-life situations. Nevertheless, this drama provides enough for us to reflect upon.

The intense effort Korean families put into preparing their children for college admissions often include negative elements as well. There are families who go all in for their children's college admissions. It includes never-ending investments of time and emotion in addition to many financial sacrifices. As family members over-focus on college admissions, their relationships can break down at times during the difficult process, especially when the desired outcomes are not achieved.

The character of Professor Minhyuk Cha in the drama particularly stood out to me. Despite being born in a poor family, he became the youngest person to pass the bar exam and eventually the youngest deputy chief prosecutor. His wife had her own doctoral degree but had given up her career to look after the family and their children's education. His daughter faked an admission to Harvard. He imposed all of his unfulfilled dreams onto his own twin sons. His conversations with his family challenge us to look back on ourselves.

The most memorable scene for me was, however, when Professor Junsang Kang lodged a complaint to his mother. He quit his job as the head of the office of planning and coordination at the university hospital and his mother confronted him about it. His mother had been proud of the fact that her son had received the highest score in the country on the Korean SAT. Her life seemed to have been focused on her son becoming the chief hospital administrator and her granddaughter going to medical school at Seoul National University to become a third-generation physician.

However, her granddaughter was forced to drop out of

high school after it was discovered that her college admission coordinator had on numerous occasions stolen test papers from the school to help her achieve higher scores. Then her son quit his job at the hospital. She ran to her son right away and berated him. Her son protested that he had never wanted to become the chief hospital administrator. He asserted that it was his mother, not he, who wanted him to become the chief administrator. He cried out, "Could I not just be your son?"

Are there not many parents who are unable to accept their children as who they are, but instead, often impose on them what they should become? Do they not also stress out their children with what to major in and what kind of jobs to hold? In their children's selection of colleges, majors, and careers, are these parents not focused more on their own desires rather than their children's aptitude and preferences? I probably had not been much different from these parents myself at one point or another while raising my own two sons. I feel sorry about it to my sons who are now all grown up.

Sex Education

Washington Media
March 24, 1999

The first time I received a sex education class was in my high school sophomore year in Korea. It was during our first biology class. The teacher put up an illustration that was not found in any of our textbooks displaying the female genital organs and explained them in detail.

I could feel the intensity in the air as it was the first time for the students to see such illustration or to hear from an adult about them. I also remember thinking that this must be what high schools were all about. However, except for what I saw and heard in that very first biology class, I had never received another lesson on sex education. I wonder how I got married and eventually produced two sons without receiving any further instruction on sex education.

I recently had a chance to meet with some friends over dinner. One of the friends had gotten married at an early age and already had a son who was a high school sophomore. He relayed to us that he had been contemplating to have a talk with his son about the use of condoms. While the son might have already received some education on it at the school, he was wondering whether it was still his fatherly duty to have a conversation.

What my friend was saying came to me as a shock at first because my first son was only a fifth grader at the time, but then the thought flashed into my mind that I might also have to face the same reality soon. Someone might argue that talking about condoms to a high school sophomore would be unwarranted. However, the percentage of high school students engaging in sex is not that low according to survey data. Therefore, this issue cannot be just ignored and overlooked.

It is true that many Korean parents including myself did not receive proper sex education when growing up. There may even be parents who have no knowledge at all that the sex education exists. As a school board member, I have been fortunate to encounter and have the chance to review the contents of sex education curriculum in public schools at least once a year. Otherwise, I could very well also be almost ignorant on sex education myself.

The debate on the pros and cons of sex education in public schools has been around for a long time. Some parents still oppose it, as they claim that it should be done at home by parents and not in schools.

I fully agree that the parents must take on the responsibility of teaching their children. However, I doubt whether all parents are adequately prepared to teach on the subject. I personally would be too embarrassed to even open a conversation. I do not even have enough knowledge on the subject to teach well, either. What's more, I do not see any harm in our children obtaining this kind of life education through their schools.

As to the morality of engaging in sex, it should be the responsibility of parents to instill in their children the values they desire. The inappropriateness of engaging in sex by students is taught in schools, but there is a limit to what schools can do. Schools cannot just teach students to stop having sex, regardless of the reality of what the data show. It is wise for parents to teach the morals while still allowing the schools to provide information to students.

Sex education should not be a taboo. An open line of communication between parents and children is crucial in properly guiding our children. Parents need to find out what and how much their children know about sex education. The first step that I would like to suggest for the parents to do is to examine the content of the sex education being provided in schools from the upper elementary grades to their children's high school senior year.

Criteria For Good Schools

The Korea Times-Washington, D.C.
May 18, 2018

"Which high school is a good one?" As a school board member, I often receive this type of question. The intent behind the question is, in general, to find out which school sends the highest percentage of students to prestigious colleges. This question comes mostly from the people who plan to move into Fairfax County, but sometimes from long-time residents of the county as well.

A few weeks ago, I had a discussion on "good schools" with a person planning to emigrate from Korea. He already knew the names of the so-called "good schools" within this area even though he was living in Korea. He might have obtained the information from his relatives or friends living here or through internet searches. He might have also reviewed some published reports on school evaluation or average SAT scores.

However, there are diverse perspectives on what defines a good school. Some may be satisfied with a school that can send their children to a highly reputable state college, while some others may not be satisfied unless their children get to go to an Ivy League college. For a particular family, the focus may instead be the chance of its child's acceptance to a prestigious college rather than the overall quality of the school.

There are some differences in the average SAT scores or the acceptance rates to colleges amongst the high schools in Fairfax County. However, it is also clear that there is not much difference in the school curricula or the quality of teachers. The only difference is in the academic achievements by students, and the reasons for these observed differences come down to individual differences between the students themselves and not necessarily the schools.

There is a strong correlation between a student's academic achievement and their parents' education level and financial ability. Consequently, academic achievements by the students from wealthy families or highly educated parents are generally higher. In contrast, when controlling for those more prominent factors, a particular student's academic achievement does not change based on which high school the student attends.

So, whenever I am asked about selecting a good high school, I emphasize the importance of the student's hard work rather than focusing on the school itself. I also often share that even though the high school that I attended in the U.S. had a high percentage of the families in poverty or of ethnic minorities, I was still accepted to good colleges.

As for recent immigrant students who must learn English as a second language, I often expound on the needs to create an environment that will promote more opportunities for them to learn English as quickly as possible. If a student lacks sufficient English language skills, he will also likely struggle in all other classes as well.

I came to the U.S. in the middle of my high school years, and my English was poor. As such, studying in the high school and preparing for college were hard. Luckily for me, there was only one other Korean student besides me at the first high school that I attended—it was more than forty years ago and there were not many Koreans living in the area at that time. So, I had no choice but to bump into native speakers at school. That is how I was able to learn English a little faster.

There has been an increase in the size of the Korean population in the Washington, D.C. area over the past forty years, and there are also many schools that have a high number of Korean students. A student who arrives recently from Korea can easily spend much of his time with the other Korean-speaking students, thereby negatively affecting his opportunities to learn and practice English language skills. Therefore, I often suggest to the new families from

Korea to choose schools with fewer Korean students and point out the importance of making friends with native speakers.

Another point to consider is to pick schools with relatively lower overall student academic achievement so that it becomes easier for the new student to stand out. In that way, you can also obtain good recommendation letters from your teachers, which will help you more in applying for colleges. This is something newly immigrated Korean students aiming for prestigious colleges should consider seriously.

Special Education

The Korea Times-Washington, D.C.
November 9, 2012

I had a chance to talk with a special education teacher some time ago. I wanted to hear from a front-line teacher. This teacher said that Korean parents generally seemed to lack enthusiasm for special education compared to the other parents. Therefore, she often hesitates to make recommendations to Korean parents to have their children screened for eligibility, even when she feels that the children may potentially benefit from special education.

According to a report published last December, approximately fourteen percent of the students in the Fairfax County public schools are currently enrolled in special education.[41] However, when you look at the racial breakdown, the percentage of Asian students is low—less than half of the percentage of Asian students comprising the overall student population. Assuming that there is no particular reason why Asian students inherently differ from non-Asian students in their needs for special education, it may be due to the difference in the Asian families' perspectives on special education.

Special education in the U.S. is provided per federal mandates under the Individuals with Disabilities Education Act (IDEA). There are several different categories for special education. In addition to programs that assist students with physical challenges, there are also services available for students with autism, learning disabilities, intellectual disabilities, emotional disorders, and attention deficit disorders, to name a few.

A student's special education service is determined based on

41 The 2020 data show 14.5 percent.

the student's Individualized Education Program (IEP). An IEP is developed by a team of experts and teachers, including the parents of the student. The team reviews the student's curriculum, academic achievement, and classroom behaviors.

An eligible student can also receive vocational education and social-emotional adaptation trainings until the age of twenty-one through his IEP, which is reviewed and adjusted annually. Unlike students in general education, special education students can receive services even during the summer breaks.

Some services are offered through outside contractors when public schools are unable to provide them. If parents are not happy with their child's IEP, there is an appeal process through which they can file their objections and have their objections adjudicated. Judicial remedies can be sought, too.

According to an analysis of the data, a proportionally higher percentage of the students receiving free or reduced-price meals are represented in special education. However, I also recollect reading a few years ago another study which indicated a proportionally higher percentage of students from the families with high levels of parental income and education receiving special education. That study did not contain analyses for the underlying reasons, but we may surmise that parents with higher income and educational levels are presumably more aggressive in pursuing ways to meet the needs of their children's education. These parents are viewing special education not as something to shun from, but instead as valuable benefit they should provide to their children.

In fact, some of the accommodations provided to students in special education can have a direct impact on the students' grades. For example, depending on the IEP, additional time can be provided for test taking. These students would be provided with additional amount of time to work on completing their tests after school without having to worry about time restrictions while the other students must finish the exam within the set time frame. Additional time can even be given to taking SATs which may affect the student's college admissions.

Of course, the needs for these types of accommodations must be based on the IEP developed with supporting evidence. Such evidence cannot be manufactured overnight, and parents should thoroughly prepare them in advance of the IEP discussion. I am not in any way indicating that parents should seek special education for their children for this purpose only. However, what I am emphasizing is that the parents should seek all necessary services without hesitation so that their children can receive the proper education they deserve.

As parents, we all have the solemn responsibilities to do our best for our children's education. School systems allocate a large amount of resource to provide special education. Parents should not avoid special education offerings for their children just because they are worried about any potential stigma. Otherwise, you are abandoning your parental duties.

Importance Of Words

The Korea Times–Washington, D.C.
May 17, 2019

I attended my younger son's graduation from graduate school last Friday and will also be going to my older son's this coming Monday. Numerous graduation ceremonies are lined up for the next month that I plan to attend as a school board member. I would like to applaud all graduating seniors and their parents and friends who have supported the graduates' hard work.

Attending my younger son's graduation, I was reminded of the importance of our words. I would like to share something that occurred when my second son was in high school. He took AP Physics during his junior year. His physics teacher was notorious for being hard, and my son struggled throughout the whole year. He often had to stay up until the wee hours of the night to work on his assignments. At times he received poor grades, which tremendously bothered him. While he was ultimately able to receive an A as his final grade for the subject, to my son, there was no other class as difficult.

In the beginning of his senior year, my younger son was working on his college applications. One day, he met his physics teacher by chance in a hallway of the school. My son greeted him and was about to pass him by. That was when he was stopped by the teacher.

The teacher then asked why my son had not asked him for a college recommendation letter. My son responded that he did not think that he had done well in his class. "You did not suck at it," the teacher replied. He was surprised by what he had heard because it was considered a compliment for that teacher. My son then asked for a recommendation letter and eventually ended

At a graduation for Thomas Jefferson High School for Science and Technology (TJ) where both of my sons attended[1]

1 My sons' AP physics teacher is on the top right; the one next to me is my sons' Latin teacher; and the one in front is my second son's guidance counselor.

up majoring in physics in college. He continued with physics in graduate school and eventually received his Ph.D.

His case proved how important our words could be. My son might not have spent ten years of his life studying physics had he never heard those encouraging words from his teacher. There were other subjects that he also liked and could have otherwise pursued for further study. The encouragement from a respected teacher had the biggest influence on his choice of field of study and his future career path.

However, the impact words can have is not always positive. In some cases, you end up regretting your whole life for spitting out the wrong words. It is more common to see the harm done by making mistakes with our words than the benefits produced from speaking well. People are often eager to criticize or insult others but can be stingy with their praises. It is more so for a person like me, a lawyer and a school board member, who must talk a lot in public daily.

I admit that I have made mistakes during meetings, although I have tried to be careful. Pointing out a mistake or criticizing someone should be avoided as much as possible, especially when staff are present at a public meeting. However, I made mistakes at times by failing to control my own desires to sound sharp or score political points. Sure, I try to apologize whenever I realize these mistakes, but these apologies often come too late due to pride or being too conscious of others being around. I keep reminding myself not to forget that I am not necessarily superior to the staff who report to me and that the only difference between us is the respective roles that we have been given.

Mistakes can also take different forms—not only in oral communications, but also in emails, text messages, and comments on social media. A wise piece of advice is not to send an email or a text message, or to write a comment on the social media, when you are too emotional. If you must send an email, complete the content but leave out the recipient's address so that you can review it later after your emotions have subsided. Otherwise, more likely than not, you will end up regretting what you have sent. Another piece of advice is to count to ten if you must speak while emotional. That way, you can give your intense emotions a chance to cool down.

Scripture says, "Consider what a great forest is set on fire by a small spark" (James 3:5). It is a warning for us to always bcar in mind that a mistake of even a single word has the potential to bring about a disaster.

Hiring Process For A New Superintendent

The Korea Times-Washington, D.C.
November 18, 2016

Dr. Karen Garza, the first female superintendent in the 150-year history of the Fairfax County Public Schools, is leaving for Columbus, Ohio. Her last day at work will be next Wednesday. She has accomplished a great deal during her relatively short tenure of three and a half years.

The two biggest achievements are the full-day Mondays for elementary schools and the later start times for high schools. Both changes required additional resources, but she accomplished them even amid tight budgets due to the economic downturn. I look forward to her new role as the CEO of a think tank that can influence the education system of our entire country. I am also thankful for the dedication she has shown to the students in Fairfax County, not necessarily an easy place to work given the high expectations the community always places on its superintendent.

Just like in most other school districts in the country, the selection process for a new superintendent exclusively falls under the responsibility of the school board.[42] Therefore, the school board started the process two months ago. The school board has already appointed the current deputy superintendent as the interim superintendent. The board also hired a retired former Fairfax County Public Schools' administrator to work as an interim deputy

42 A superintendent's contract cannot be for more than four years at any one time in Virginia. In addition, the contract for a new superintendent cannot be for less than two years. There is no limit on the number of the contract renewals, though.

superintendent until a new superintendent is hired. Once a new superintendent is hired, the interim superintendent will resume his previous deputy superintendent's position. All these steps are being taken to minimize the administrative gap at the top for the school district.

As usual, the superintendent search is going to be done with assistance provided by an outside search firm. The school board has completed the selection process of the search firm this Monday. The firm selected is the same one that assisted the board in hiring of the immediate past two superintendents. The quality of the services rendered by this firm had been rated highly. There are only a few search firms in the country that can assist the school districts as large as Fairfax County in hiring superintendents.

The hiring process for a superintendent takes longer than what people may think. It took almost a year last time. The school board had enough time the last time to go through the search process because the former superintendent had given the school board a notice of his intention to retire nine months in advance. However, the resignation of the current superintendent was unexpected and has put the school board in a situation of having to rush. Although there is an interim superintendent, hiring a new superintendent as quickly as possible will help to maintain the stability within the school system's administration from its central office.

Fortunately, this search firm is quite familiar with Fairfax County Public Schools. Also, the process will be much faster this time as the firm could refer to the same materials used four years ago. For example, this firm conducted a survey and collected feedback from the residents and various interest groups on the qualities they were seeking in the new superintendent four years ago—I do not think the opinions of the residents would have changed greatly since then. Therefore, the process of collecting feedback could be shorter this time.

The current board has more members with superintendent hiring experience, too. Last time, only four of the twelve members had experience with such a process, but there are eight this time around. Having more members with experience this time will help the board not waste time from discussing unnecessary issues that can arise from inexperience.

The first meeting with the search firm is scheduled to take place on December 1. That is when the board will discuss the timeline of the search process in detail. I hope that the board completes its process and hires a new superintendent by the end of April next year. That will provide the superintendent with sufficient time to prepare for the new job and officially start on July 1 next year, which is also the first day of a new fiscal year.

I also hope for active participation by members of the local Korean community by voicing their opinions during the search process. After all, this process is to find the best qualified person to take on the most important and influential position in the educational administration that will affect the education of our children.

The Superintendent And The Wallet

The Korea Times–Washington, D.C.
March 22, 2013

The Fairfax County School Board on which I currently serve as the chairman completed the first round of its evaluation process for hiring a new superintendent last week. The discussions took nearly twenty-five hours and spanned four days, from Thursday to Sunday.

The second round will be held during the first week in April. During the second round, there will also be interviews by the community panel consisting of eighteen teachers, parents, students, and community representatives, all appointed by the school board. The panel will have a chance to meet with the candidates and submit its evaluations of the candidates to the school board.

During the first round of interviews, as expected, the school board members asked each candidate about the candidate's view on the role of superintendent. The questions also included their views on the budget. School boards in Virginia do not have a taxing authority. Therefore, they must depend on the federal, state, and the local governments to provide its funding. In the case of Fairfax County, about seventy percent of the education budget comes from the county government.

In establishing an annual budget, the superintendent's initial budget proposal is the most critical step. It is the starting point for an annual tug-of-war between the school board wanting to secure the sufficient funding and the county board of supervisors that is responsible for raising revenue through its taxing authority.

Almost every year, the board of supervisors expresses its dissatisfaction with the budget proposal submitted by the superintendent. The supervisors routinely argue that the proposal constitutes an unreasonable demand without considering the overall revenue to the county government or the economic situation. They also often accuse that the superintendent is being selfish to think that the public education is the county's only important priority.

Often, a debate about the role of the superintendent surfaces during the budget discussion with diverse viewpoints on whether the superintendent should only focus on public education or has a responsibility to consider the county's overall budgetary needs.

As I was thinking about what budget-related questions to ask during the candidates' first round of interviews, an episode involving a wallet invoked by Dr. Daniel Domenech, the predecessor to the current superintendent Dr. Jack Dale, came to my mind.

The strong-willed Dr. Domenech always took on the role of a crusader in fighting for education funding. He believed that it was his duty as superintendent. He argued that his role was to present the financial needs of the public schools and to advocate for sufficient funding. He further claimed said that he was the superintendent of the public schools and not of the county.

Dr. Domenech's approach always bothered the chairman of the county board of supervisors. The chairman at the time was a man who himself had with a strong personality and pride, not much different from Dr. Domenech, and did not hesitate in expressing his opinions, either. Therefore, they often ended up butting heads.[43]

At a joint meeting of the school board and the board of supervisors to discuss budget issues shortly after Dr. Domenech announced his retirement in early 2004, the chairman of the board of supervisors and Dr. Domenech exchanged some sharp

---

43 Mr. Gerry Connolly, then chairman of the Board of Supervisors, was elected to Congress in November 2008 and is in his seventh term as of May 2021. Dr. Daniel Domenech is now the Executive Director of the American Association of School Administrators.

comments. That meeting was Dr. Domenech's last opportunity to discuss the budget with the supervisors.

The chairman of the board of supervisors insisted that the education funding request was excessive and argued that there surely had to be a room for reduction. He further commented that the school system should not expect to be able to do everything it wanted. He then suggested that the school system come up with a priority list of the programs it wanted to support and to consider eliminating some programs.

Dr. Domenech responded that there was no unnecessary program included in the budget proposal and any extraneous program would have been already excluded. He then pressed the supervisors to approve the submitted budget proposal as is if the supervisors believed that public education was important. He further commented to the chairman of the board of supervisors that his role as the superintendent was to "take every penny out of the chairman's wallet." Upon hearing the superintendent's comments, the chairman was unable to respond right away, with his face immediately turning dark red, seemingly both embarrassed and angry.

The wallet episode resurfaced at Dr. Domenech's retirement reception. A lot of people attended the reception. Not only those directly involved in the public schools but also many community leaders came to thank and bid farewell to him. Of course, the chairman of the board of supervisors could not skip it, either. After delivering remarks in the early part of the program, the chairman was about to leave citing another commitment he had. It was at that moment the superintendent then shouted out a joke, "Mr. Chairman, your wallet is in my hands!" The reception area was immediately filled with laughter. Sure, the chairman managed to show a smile, but it looked to be a bitter one. [44]

---

44 Dr. Domenech, to this date, has been the only Hispanic superintendent in Fairfax County. He came to the U.S. from Cuba at the age of nine and speaks Spanish fluently.

At an event with Superintendent Dr. Daniel Domenech second from the right (1999)[45]

When the school board went into a search for Dr. Domenech's successor, it surely wanted to find someone who could improve the relationship with the board of supervisors. Jury is still out on whether the current superintendent Dr. Jack Dale has been successful during his tenure in helping the school board achieve its goal of improving its relationship with the board of supervisors. Some people feel that it could have been better while there are others who argue that he has been too compliant to the board of supervisors. Nevertheless, Dr. Dale has maintained a much less awkward relationship than his predecessor.

I wonder how the next superintendent will take on the relationship challenge. I guess it might sound too textbook-like if I asked the superintendent to be nimble in dealing with the county supervisors and to be prepared to adjust between being strong and mild according to the situation. A difficulty is that one person's idea of being strong may be mild in another person's view. It is almost certain that both the current and former superintendents might have thought in their own minds that they had been nimble in balancing strong and mild strategies according to the needs of the day.

All Night Graduation Party

The Korea Times-Washington, D.C.
June 7, 2013

It is a graduation season. I have already attended two special education school graduations this week. The regular high school graduations will start next week, and I plan to attend around twenty of them. Attending graduations is exciting, fun-filled, and yet hard. I ache all over by the time the season ends as I must sit quietly on stage throughout all ceremonies.

Each school organizes a party to be held after the graduation ceremony so that the students can enjoy and celebrate in a safe environment. These parties are called "All Night Graduation Parties". The party is generally at the school or in rented public places.

Many parents volunteer to provide a successful party, and the graduates normally purchase tickets to attend. Sometimes, funds are raised to help the students who cannot afford to purchase the tickets. The organizers also receive donations of food and merchandise from local community. Plenty of foods and games are available for everyone to enjoy. Bringing in food from outside is not allowed and access to the party is strictly regulated. Of course, alcohols and drugs are strictly prohibited.

To ensure the students' safety, their parents are notified when they are about to leave the party. This is to prevent the students from going anywhere else. That is why parents can send their children to this party with a peace of mind. Most schools also prohibit graduating seniors from driving to the party themselves to prevent them from driving home when they are too tired after an all-night party.

These graduation parties require well-planned preparations and hard work—they are only possible with the cooperation of many people. Many volunteers are needed on the day of the party as well. The volunteers at the party are not the parents of the graduating students but rather the parents of the underclass students. Parents of the graduating students are normally busy and tired from hosting out of town guests and holding events like a dinner party following the graduation ceremony. Plus, these parents also must give a ride to the students attending the graduation party. Therefore, they are excluded from volunteering at the party. Moreover, the graduating students may not necessarily want to see their parents looking over their shoulders at the party, either. That is why the parents of the underclass students should volunteer.

I volunteered twice when my sons were in high school and learned that volunteering could be hard work. The first time I did, I oversaw a game for three hours and operating that game consumed quite a bit of energy. Of course, other volunteers relieved me from time to time so that I could rest. Nevertheless, it was tiring.

The second time, I was at the main entrance checking in the students coming in. My shift started in the early dawn hours and I had a tough time shaking off sleepiness. Many parents gladly volunteer, though, despite knowing that the work could be taxing on their bodies as everyone knows that such party cannot be held without parent volunteers.

Another volunteering opportunity at an all-night party came by this year. As my two own sons had already graduated from high school, I no longer felt an obligation to volunteer as a parent. However, having received an invitation to volunteer from a high school, I just accepted it.

I was informed that the casino card games were most popular amongst students, so I decided to be a dealer at a blackjack table for about two and a half hours. I received special permission to open the game table a little bit early at 10 p.m. and attended an orientation session last week to receive some card dealer training. No real money is involved, though. Fake game money is given to students in advance to use at the game tables. The winnings are then exchanged with the raffle tickets—prizes are given out by drawing raffle tickets at the end of all the games.

I have never been a blackjack dealer and am not even good at playing the game. So, I was cautious about volunteering at first. I felt more comfortable after attending the orientation session as I found out that there were many other volunteers who did not even know the basic rules of blackjack game. Besides, the game is mainly for the graduating students to simply enjoy. Therefore, no one would complain about the small mistakes I would invariably make here and there or any unintentional breaches of game rules.

In a casino dealer's uniform

Volunteering at the party, though, I felt that the party could use many more volunteers. The tasks for the party include preparation of the party hall, cleaning up afterwards, guiding in the school parking lot, and acting as security personnel. There are also simple errands to run such as carrying food around, picking up trash, etc. Of course, a photographer is needed, too.

I would like to strongly recommend to parents with high school children to volunteer as much as possible. All you must do is to contact the party preparatory committee of your school. It is still not too late. I believe that we, as parents, have the responsibility to participate in work that will benefit others, instead of only looking for the benefits that our children can take advantage of. I hope to see many Korean parents amongst the volunteers as well.

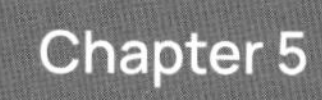

Chapter 5

Stories Of American Society

Introduction

I am simultaneously living in two different cultures of two countries, keeping many traditions of my childhood home of Korea where I was born and lived until I was 17, and embracing new traditions from my adopted home in the U.S.A.

Of course, cultures can change. It may also be difficult to pinpoint what exactly constitutes "American culture" in a country like the U.S. where people from diverse backgrounds live together. It is not about whether a particular culture is superior or inferior. Furthermore, there is no mandate for anyone to live according to American culture just because he or she is living in the U.S. It does not matter how we live as long as we are happy and do not harm others.

Then again, it is perfectly fine for one to learn from another culture if learning such culture will be beneficial. When certain behaviors or traits from another culture make you feel uncomfortable, try to learn and understand people's backgrounds so that conflicts can be avoided.

This was something I learned the hard way quite a while ago. I wanted to give small Christmas gifts to some business associates who had been helpful to my law practice. I remembered how my father used to bring home a Christmas ham given out by his employer during my high school days when I first came to the U.S. They tasted so good, especially when roasted in oven.

Following suit, I ordered hams in a large quantity and gave them out. I continued this ritually for a few years. Then, one year, someone who had been regularly receiving the hams from me asked me not to send them to any other person in her office. They were all Muslims and therefore did not eat pork. It had never crossed my mind and I felt so embarrassed.

Another episode that I wanted to share occurred when my

younger son was little. There was an occasion that required me to lecture and reprimand him. He was looking at me straight in the eyes while I was talking to him. A question came to my mind, "How dare was he looking at me that way when his father was addressing the issue?" Then, I quickly remembered that thc schools in the U.S. taught students to look adults in the eyes when they speak. I almost chuckled.

In Korean, *hyung* means "older brother", but my younger son still calls his older brother *hyung-ah*, the same way he used to call him when they both were little boys. Someone pointed out to my younger son that *hyung-ah* was a word used by small children, but my son has not been able to change his old habit to this date.

I guess that is the most comfortable way for him to call his older brother. If he were like most other American-born children, he would just call his older brother by the first name—but, in that case, his older brother might consider that to be rude.[45] I still feel awkward calling someone by his or her first name and feel the same when someone calls me by my first name when we are not that close to each other.

---

45 Upon reading this, my first son commented that he was not sure whether he would say that it was rude, but it would feel strange at first. He then added, "I actually told an older Korean student at Harvard who demanded to be called "*hyung*" that he refused and would call him by his first name. I think he was taken aback at first but then got over it and realized we'd have an "American-style" friendship instead of the Korean type that came with strings attached."

Hamburger Coke

The Korea Times-Washington D.C.
January 6, 2012

I met a custodial supervisor when I visited a high school on business a few days ago. He greeted me at the door with warmth when I was about to leave after the meeting. He seemed to be an African immigrant. I could not remember who he was, but I greeted him, too, anyway. Then he told me that he remembered my "hamburger story". It was a story that I had shared at an event about thirteen years ago—I was pleasantly surprised that he still remembered it.

The Fairfax County public school system had developed a training program for school custodians who were English-language learners and wanted to pursue professional growth. At a ceremony held thirteen years ago to congratulate custodians who had completed the training, I told a story about hamburgers. It was a story I had heard from somewhere else, and I thought that the story was appropriate for the occasion.

The story was of a new immigrant to the U.S. He did not have any job skills but luckily got a job as a construction helper. He did not speak much English. The only English words that he learned before coming to the U.S. and felt comfortable saying were "hamburger" and "coke". He had somehow heard that "cola" was called "coke" in the U.S.

He packed his lunch at first but saw the other workers buying hamburgers. He wanted to save every penny, so he could not afford to buy a hamburger for himself. His co-workers then tempted him saying how delicious the hamburgers were. He finally gave in and decided to try one, of course, with a coke.

On one day, he lined up with the other workers in front of the hamburger restaurant to buy a hamburger. The line was quite long. He practiced his order, repeating "hamburger, coke" while waiting in line. He was finally able to purchase a hamburger and a coke, and the taste was utterly amazing, just like what everyone had told him. It was like the old saying that "it was so good that you would not notice even if the person eating with you died." So, he went back to buy a hamburger again the next day. The same continued on the following day and so on. The hamburger was so delicious, and he was not getting tired of eating the same food every day.

After a while, though, he wanted to try something slightly different. He had heard about the wonders of the "cheeseburger". Someone told him that hamburger would taste even better with a slice of cheese included. He wanted to give it a try. His English skills had improved a bit by then, and he felt that he could order a cheeseburger without a problem.

He practiced "cheeseburger, coke" while waiting in line. He thought that he must communicate clearly to the person taking orders as that person had been accustomed to his orders of hamburger. His heart was pounding as he was getting closer to the counter. The excitement of trying a new food and the anxiety of having to use a new English word intertwining.

When he finally reached the counter, he was asked, as usual, what he wanted to order. He quickly answered, "cheeseburger, coke." He thought that he answered it loudly. However, his voice must have been soft, perhaps because he was so nervous. The counter person asked again, "what's your order?" That startled him, and he lost his confidence. "No, hamburger, coke." Back to the same old order. He ended up having a hamburger and a coke for lunch again that day. Legend goes, to this date, he is still buying a hamburger and a coke for lunch every day.

This is probably not a true story, but it portrays the sorrow and struggle of people not able to pursue their dreams or fully utilize their capabilities after coming to the U.S. as immigrants due to inadequate English skills or the unfamiliar setting.

I wanted to share this story to encourage those who might

find themselves in a similar situation. No one should ever give up ordering a cheeseburger when they certainly are able to order one. Life as an immigrant can be challenging, but let us not lose confidence without even trying. Let us not waste our potentials without making earnest efforts to use them well. Let us not miss out on opportunities to grow wherever we are. Instead, let us aggressively seek out those opportunities.

Making remarks to school custodians (circa 1999)

Los Angeles Riots
-The Twenty-Fifth Anniversary

The Korea Times-Washington D.C.
May 5, 2017

Last Saturday was the twenty-fifth anniversary of the Los Angeles Riots. Those living in the Washington, D.C. area spent the day quietly unlike the Korean community in the Los Angeles area. However, we should never forget the riots, considering the shock that the riots brought to us and their root causes. We need to remember, and teach our future generations, the lessons learned from the riots.

That is why I have been talking about the Los Angeles Riots to my high school freshman classes in my church on the Sunday right before April 29 for the past several years. I explained the background of the riots and shared some video clips showing the scenes of the riots at the time and the people reflecting on their experiences of the riots.

Sure, these videos clips may not be related to the Bible study. However, I feel the need to provide opportunities for students, at least the students in my care, to learn the nature of the riots, considering the importance of the role played by churches within the Korean community and the challenges that the riots present to all Christians.

The Los Angeles Riots started on April 29, 1992, and lasted for five days. The riots resulted in the fifty deaths, injuries to thousands of people, and property damages totaling over one billion dollars. Most of all, the Korean community suffered the most damages. Despite this history, hardly any of the students in my classes over the last several years had heard about the riots.

There may be many Korean adults who are not familiar about it, either.

The riots occurred twenty-five years ago in 1992; therefore, young students, as well as newer immigrants, may not know about them. Still, some may have had the chance to learn and think about them through media coverage around the anniversary of the riots each year. Regardless, we should never just pass the anniversary when we know that the Korean community was, in fact, the biggest victim.

Among the video clips that I have been sharing with my students is the one showing an outcry by K.W. Lee, a longtime Korean American journalist well known to mainstream media. He emphatically argues in the video that the future path of the Korean American community must be determined and developed by Korean Americans themselves and should never be left in the hands of the mainstream media or politicians who do not know them well enough.

Another video shows a young Korean photographer working for the Los Angeles Times at the time reminiscing about the sightings of the riots. He points out in the video that Koreans were not the only victims.

The direct fuse for the riots was the non-guilty verdict handed down by a majority-white jury in the trial of the four white police officers who had mercilessly beaten Rodney King, an African American, a year earlier. However, it was bizarre how the Korean community became the target of the riots. The demonstrators originally headed for a white-dominated area, but, when they could not break through the police blockage, they then moved to the Koreatown, a commercial district where many stores were owned by Koreans.

Some claim that that the conflicts that had existed under the surface between the Korean and African American communities had finally exploded. An appeal by the prosecutors' office in the case of the death of a fifteen-year-old black girl shot and killed by a Korean store owner had been dismissed only a week prior to the riots. The seemingly light sentence given out by the trial court and the subsequent dismissal of the prosecution's appeal by the superior court might have kindled a fire in the African American community.

However, the root causes for all these conflicts still mainly stem from the African American community's inability to escape from poverty, unemployment, and low education. All these causes still exist, and not much has changed for the past twenty years although we even had an African American president.

Of course, we could debate about who should take the responsibility for these outcomes. Unless a reasonable measure to solve the above-described fundamental problems is established, the Los Angeles riots will not be just a one-time incident that happened twenty-five years ago but will continue to be an ongoing issue. It is an active volcano waiting to erupt above the ground at any time. Therefore, we must focus on finding the true solutions in addition to educating future generations about them as well. As K W. Lee claimed, we cannot just leave our fate to others.

At The News Of Arrests Of Undocumented Immigrants

The Korea Times-Washington D.C.
February 17, 2017

I received a text message from a fellow school board member last Friday evening. Mentioning the crackdown of undocumented immigrants in the Annandale and Alexandria areas by the officers of Immigration and Customs Enforcement (ICE), Department of Homeland Security, she asked me whether I could provide any further detail. After hearing my response that I had nothing to provide, she messaged me again with the news that some were arrested, while others narrowly escaped the arrests, because of the presence of young children at the scene.

Another board member relayed the information that the parking lots of the apartment complexes where many low-income immigrants lived were completely empty now and that President Trump must be carrying out his election pledge of massive deportation of undocumented immigrants. This board member further said that most of all, he was worried about the students and concerned that ICE might come to schools.

While exchanging these text messages, I remembered an old Korean friend from the high school I had attended in Alexandria, Virginia. He wanted to be a medical doctor and studied hard. He often worked part time as a security guard on weekends at the same company where his father worked. With the money he earned, he chipped in for his family's living expenses and saved some for college.

We were quite close to each other and talked a lot about studying and our future aspirations. By the end of the winter of our senior year, we were almost done with our decisions on which colleges to attend. We also agreed to visit Korea together during the summer break before going off to college. It was exciting—I worked part time to earn money for the trip, and we developed detailed plans for things to do together in Korea.

As the graduation was fast approaching, it was time to purchase the plane tickets. However, my friend hesitated and said that he was not quite ready but did not disclose a clear explanation as to why. When I urged him later that we could not delay the ticket purchase any longer, he finally confessed the fact that he did not have a green card. He would not be able come back to the U.S. if he went to Korea.

My heart was breaking. How anxious he must have been about his status all these years and how much longer he still must suffer. How hard it must have been for him whenever I showed my excitement for the upcoming visit to our homeland. I could not come up with a word that could console him. Fortunately, my friend and his whole family eventually obtained their green cards, and he realized his aspiration of becoming a medical doctor. I was delighted and grateful that everything turned out fine for him.[46]

What would have happened to him if he had been arrested as an undocumented immigrant at that time? He, as well as his parents and siblings, could have been deported to Korea. He might even have had to give up his studies as he might not have been able to overcome the academic differences between the high schools in Korea and the U.S. It would also have been difficult for his parents to find jobs in Korea, and the family would have suffered a great deal financially.

46 He has two children with one teaching in a medical school and another pursuing a legal career.

With the friend who was an undocumented immigrant at the time
in front of his college dorm (1977)

I have been serving as a board member in Fairfax County for the past eighteen years. I have often witnessed the reactions of our residents on issues related to immigrant students. I have always approached discussions around those issues with more sensitivity, perhaps because I am not only a board member but also an immigrant myself. I find it difficult to strictly separate the issues related to undocumented immigrants from those of legal immigrants.

Why do so many undocumented immigrants stay in the U.S., living in fear instead of returning to their home countries? In many instances, it might be poverty. Although the U.S. has not completely recovered from the economic downturn yet, it cannot be compared to the kinds of difficulties that the deported immigrants may have to face if forced to return to their home countries.

I immigrated to the U.S. in the middle of my high school years to escape from poverty and to seek a better life. There is no difference between most of undocumented immigrants from South and Central America and me. Therefore, I cannot sweep it aside as someone else's story when I hear a story about someone getting deported.

I also question whether such an extreme measure of deportation is truly in line with the Christian spirit, especially because this country was founded based on Christian roots. Is the mission to care for the hungry, the naked, and the sick only limited for the legal immigrants and citizens in a country that claims seventy to eighty percent of its citizens as Christians?

Two Proud Korean Police Officers

The Korea Times-Washington D.C.
August 3, 2018

The Fairfax County School Board discussed the memorandum of understanding (MOU) for its program for school resource officers (SRO) last Thursday evening. The MOU is between the Fairfax County Public Schools and the Fairfax County Police Department. The current MOU entered in 2014 needed to be revised and updated. There was also a consensus that it would be good to use the standard form recommended for the entire State of Virginia.

The SRO program was instituted to ensure the safety of the students and teachers as well as to provide crime prevention education for students. This program first emerged in the U.S. in the 1970s, but for Fairfax County, they did not appear until the 1990s in a few high schools. Since then, it has grown to now being in all middle and high schools within the county, with each school having one police officer assigned. There are currently fifty-one SROs and three supervisors across the county's schools.

The number of SROs in Fairfax County has increased since 2004, and the main reason for the increase was to deal with the rising youth gang problems. The school system has witnessed sharp increases in gang violence and forced entry into gang membership at the schools. Most of the funding needed for the program is borne by the county government. Only a small portion comes from federal grants. There is no funding from the school system.

The entire process surrounding the discussion about the MOU

revision has not been easy. After all, any change means altering the practices that have been in place for over ten years. For example, there was a demand to restrict the police officers' access to student information since they continue to play a role in criminal law enforcement. An agreement was reached that an outside police officer would take over when criminal penalties were charged or investigations were underway, except in the case of active crimes.

It was also decided to prohibit the involvement of SROs in student discipline for violating school regulations. It has been further agreed to apply school regulations and not criminal codes in taking disciplinary actions. Moreover, the disciplinary consequences would focus on inducing changes in behaviors and attitudes based upon the principles of restorative justice, instead of being punitive in nature.

As the MOU was going to be signed by the Chief of the Police Department and the Superintendent of the school system, they mostly led the negotiations and discussions. However, the Superintendent had regularly provided progress reports to the school board and sought input from the board members, especially because the MOU discussion became a politically sensitive issue.

A big challenge emerged towards the end of the process, and it was on the question of whether to report undocumented immigrant students to ICE. Several human rights organizations in the community insisted that the Police Department and the school administrators should not release information about students or cooperate with ICE. They further requested that this agreement must be explicitly spelled out in the memorandum.

It is already a policy of the school system not to release student information to ICE. In addition, the school system does not inquire or possess the immigration status information of any student. Therefore, there is no information available for ICE, even if requested. It is also the position of the Police Department not to comply with such requests from ICE. However, neither the school system nor the Police Department can refuse to comply with an arrest or search warrant issued by a court or any order from judges.

Noncompliance with a court's decision is contrary to the rule of law.

The police chief attended a closed meeting of the school board and answered the questions from board members last Thursday. Accompanying the chief at the time were two high-ranking police officers who both happened to be Korean Americans. They were the highest-ranking Korean police officers in the county. They even remained in attendance for the regular public meeting after the closed meeting has ended to provide answers to more questions from the board members in public. I felt immensely proud of the two officers. I have no doubt that they would become excellent role models for the younger generation considering a job in the police.[47]

47 On September 20, 2018, about six weeks after the publication of this column, Mr. Gun Lee, on the far right, was promoted to become one of the three Deputy Chiefs. Tonny Kim has been promoted and is now one of the Commanders in the Fairfax County Police Department.

Deputy Police Chief Gun Lee on the right
and Captain Tonny Kim in the middle

Washington House Story

The Korea Times-Washington D.C.
May 10, 2019

I attended a Cinco de Mayo party last Sunday night. Cinco de Mayo means May 5th in Spanish, and it is said that it was established to commemorate the defeat of the French invasion by Mexico at the Battle of Puebla in 1862. It is now celebrated as a cultural event for Mexicans living in the U.S., more so than in their home country, Mexico.

Mexico ran into enormous foreign debts resulted from the war with the U.S. during 1846-1848 and a subsequent civil war. In 1861, the Mexican government unilaterally announced the suspension of payments of interest on the foreign debts for two years as the government had run out of money.

France demanded repayment of the debts and eventually invaded Mexico. Mexico was losing the battle at first but defeated the French army at the Battle of Puebla with a much smaller military force. The French army attacked Mexico again the following year and stayed in Mexico until retreating in 1867 under pressure from the U.S. To Mexicans, the Battle of Puebla became a symbol of pride for winning against a powerful European country.

Coincidentally, the Cinco de Mayo party that I attended was held at what used to be called the Washington House, known as a social gathering place for the local Korean American community. The Washington House, which used to be located on Columbia Pike, Falls Church, no longer exists. However, it had been one of the few taverns with live bands in the Korean American community for many years. It was a place where many Korean immigrants could have a drink and listen to the music that reminded them of the homeland. Of course, they would also share the difficulties of immigrant life and exchange information.

My parents had been there many times as well. There was a dance floor right in front of the band. My parents visited the place with a social group of friends. The group met about once a month and learned ballroom dancing. The dance lessons werc normally held at a member's house, but the Washington House provided a venue to practice what they learned.

The members of the social group were not well off financially. Men would order one or two bottles of beer, but the women mostly ordered a soda and then danced for two to three hours. They usually took the best tables right in front of the band. The owner of the Washington House never complained about the group taking the best seats without boosting sales. The owner fully understood the financial situations of their fellow countrymen. People were grateful for his kind heart.

How the Washington House looks today

During the winter break of my senior year in college, there was an occasion for me to visit the place with two of my friends. None of us had a girlfriend at the time. We sat down and were having conversation when we noticed a beautiful, young woman sitting alone at a table not too far away. She caught our attention and we bet on who would be the first one to approach and talk to her. I courageously raised my hand first and then went over to her table. She appeared to be a student upon closer look. I sat down beside her without permission and asked her whether she was a student. She said "yes." I asked her what grade she was in. "Junior year in high school." I was suddenly lost for words.

The next question that came to my mind was to ask whether a high school student could come to a place like this. She responded that she came with her parents. I then quickly looked around, only to notice that a couple of middle aged people on the dance floor were looking at us seemingly with suspicion. I somehow needed to find a way to end the conversation on a good note. The only thing that I could think of was giving out an unsolicited advice on college application process. I told her to study hard before quickly returning to my table. My friends could not stop laughing upon hearing the whole story.

That was forty years ago. The tables and walls were imprinted with the memories of the warm conversations and stories of my fellow countrymen. But now, it is the Latinx community that is continuing many of the same conversations and stories. The Latinx community is the group living in the worst conditions in many aspects among the immigrants in the U.S. I pray that they will carry through their lives well, even if it is not so easy at this moment.

Role Of Korean Churches

The Korea Times-Washington D.C.
February 26, 2016

An article in a Korean community newspaper last week caught my attention. It was titled "Korean church is an isolated island"—it reflected exactly what I had been thinking. The article referenced a lecture by Rev. Chan Hyuk Lim, a missionary at the Billy Graham Center who had immigrated to the U.S. when he was a teenager in 1980.

I wanted to read the full text of his lecture, so I sent an email to him after finding his contact information on the website of the mission center. Thankfully, he sent me the full text of the lecture without hesitation. In the closing words of his lecture, Rev. Lim states:

> *The Korean diaspora churches in North America give an appearance of an outsider among the churches as if it were a lonely island floating on water. It is now necessary to escape from their status and establish an open dialogue, unity, and cooperation with the other ethnic churches and mission agencies within America. (...)*
>
> *We need to connect with more mainstream churches and organizations and be more focused on learning and sharing. We, the Korean diaspora churches appearing like isolated islands in the sea of North America, must cross the boundary of the Korean line, serve the local community, be interested in the multi-ethnic/multi-cultural ministries, and actively participate in the re-*

evangelization of North America. (...)

If the Korean churches in North America remained as "Korean islands" in the twenty-first century, they would continue to be isolated and gradually deteriorate, and their influence would be diminished in the future.

I have been attending Korean churches since I immigrated to the U.S. during my high school years forty years ago. I have attended American churches a few times, but I have never joined one. It is amazing that there are approximately five thousand Korean churches in North America.

As these churches have become the focal point in the Korean community, I do not need to reiterate the importance of their roles. Not only in terms of faith but also as the center of the immigrant society, these churches play the role of providing a space where Korean immigrants come to share their joy and hardships, console each other, and exchange information. They also act as the places to teach Korean culture and language to the second and the third generations born here in the U.S.

The potential that these Korean churches possess is enormous. As immigrants generally have pioneering spirits and are hard-working, the churches they attend are never in short supply of human resources compared to the other community organizations. These immigrants are also quite religious and faithful in their commitments to their churches. Many of them spend a lot of time in their churches even amid their busy lives.

Many Korean churches have worship services several times a week, including early morning worship services, which is rare for non-Korean churches in the U.S. Members' financial commitment to their churches is remarkably high as well. That is why we can take a deep pride in our Korean churches.

However, on the other hand, we cannot deny the existence of certain adverse effects from Korean churches, either. As Rev. Lim pointed out, the entire Korean community could also be isolated from the community at large if the resources of the Korean community were concentrated in these churches, appearing like an island in an ocean called North America.

I have been serving in public office for the past twenty years while working as an attorney at the same time—four years were on the Fairfax County Planning Commission and almost seventeen years as a member of the school board. During those years, I have had chance to take a close look at how the mainstream community works and how its members participate in community activities. I have also learned what types of residents take more active roles and how influential they become in their community affairs or projects where volunteers and community inputs are needed.

Regrettably, only a small fraction of Koreans step outside the fence of the Korean community although the community is full of abundant human resources. Korean churches, where these human resources are concentrated, may be responsible for this. Korean churches should be more courageous and generous. They must free the resources they have. If the Korean immigrant community appears isolated like an island, Korean churches should not then deepen such isolation but, instead, must act as a bridge connecting it to the land.

The Korean United Methodist Church of Greater Washington [48]
(Photo provided by David Huisup Hwang)

48 This is the church I have been attending since 1988. It is currently located in McLean, Virginia. The church was established in 1951 in the Washington, D.C. as the first Korean church in the Washington, D.C. area. The current main sanctuary on the far right was built in 1998. The Wesley Wing, which is on the left side of the building, was renovated in 2021.

A Cup Of Coffee On Credit

The Korea Times-Washington D.C.
July 7, 2017

I had a cup of coffee on credit at McDonald's last Saturday morning. It was the first time that I ate or drank anything on credit. Many thoughts about the credit came across while I was having the coffee.

I often stop by this McDonald's. It is at a perfect distance from my house for my walk on weekend mornings. I use it as the turning point. I normally carry a bottle of water and an empty tumbler in a small backpack whenever I go for a walk toward the McDonald's. I drink the water when I get thirsty, but what I enjoy the most is getting a cup of coffee to drink at the turning-point McDonald's. I always put the coffee into the tumbler that I carry. I also became qualified for a senior discount a few years ago, so coffee became that much cheaper as well! Drinking hot coffee out of the tumbler on the way back home from the McDonald's while listening to some music from my phone is just so much fun.

I walked to the McDonald's last Saturday morning as usual. I found out that I did not bring my wallet when I was about to buy coffee. I normally put enough change in my pocket for coffee even when I do not carry the wallet. But, somehow, I left home with an empty pocket that morning. I could have skipped the coffee for once, but I craved it even more that morning, perhaps because I did not have any money on me. I looked around inside the McDonald's to see whether there was anyone that I knew. No familiar faces. I then decided to try something that I had never done before: to ask whether I could get a cup of coffee on credit.

I asked for the manager as I thought that the counter clerk probably could not approve a credit sale no matter how small the amount was. I introduced myself as a loyal customer to the manager who came to the counter even though she was busy. I asked her whether I could get a cup of coffee on a promise to come back later that day and pay for it. It was quite embarrassing that I forgot to bring my wallet. The manager looked at me for a moment and then asked me what size I wanted. I told her that a small size for seniors would be fine. Well, I managed to get the coffee and thanked the manager. I transferred the coffee into my tumbler and walked back home while drinking coffee and listening to music as usual.

Walking back home, I asked myself what I would have done if I were the manager. How would I have responded had it been more than just a cup of coffee and included a full meal as well? What would have been the criteria for my decisions? Thinking about the manager's kindness, I realized that even though it was just a cup of coffee this time, there had been many other things that I had received on credit in my life.

There was once a teacher who gave me an expensive set of books to read. There were many senior alums from the same schools that I had graduated from and other older people who had bought me meals. A couple had lent me money without any interest so that I could open my law practice. All those many supporters who had sent me campaign donations whenever I ran for election. The volunteers who put up campaign signs, voters who lined up early in the morning to cast votes for me, and the people who gave me warm words of encouragement when I was stressed out or felt tired working as a school board member. I am deeply indebted to all of them, and I wonder whether and how I have repaid them properly. If I have not, I must find ways to do it somehow.

As promised, I went back to that McDonald's on the Saturday with seventy-three cents worth of coins. However, the same manager was not there anymore perhaps because I came late. I explained the situation to the manager on duty at that point and tried to hand over the money. That manager refused to take the money and told me not to worry it as a cup of coffee could be given out free anyway. I gave up after a few more attempts and returned home.

The next morning, I went back and found the same manager working. She looked busy, so I waited standing next to a front counter until she came forward. She remembered me when I greeted her. I handed her the exact change for coffee and she accepted it with a smile. My heart felt lighter.

As I was turning around, a mischievous thought visited me for a split second. Should I go back and ask for another cup of coffee on credit?

A Conversation With A Homeless Person

The Korea Times-Washington D.C.
March 16, 2018

I had a chance to talk to a homeless person last Saturday in Washington D.C. I had seen homeless people from time to time, but I had seldom talked to them. I had an earnest conversation this time, though.

This was the second time that I talked to a homeless individual. The first time was about thirty years ago. I happened to see a hitchhiker near a highway entrance on my way back home to Virginia from Baltimore, Maryland. I decided to give him a ride. When he got into a car, I could tell right away that he was homeless, and fear suddenly came over me. He sat in the back seat as my wife was sitting in the passenger seat in the front. I got worried with the thought of what would happen if he took out a weapon and harmed me and my wife. He could have turned into a robber due to financial hardships or mental illness. However, I could not tell him to get out of the car—it was too late.

The homeless hitchhiker told me that he was headed to Washington, D.C. I did not have to go through there but decided to take him there since I was already giving him a ride. Besides, it would take him a long time to get there if he had to walk. It was an hour drive by car. We talked a lot on the way. I asked him why he was going to Washington, D.C., and he responded that the living condition was better there. It had never occurred to me that the living conditions of the homeless could be different depending upon the location. He was making a big move in search for a better life, even as a homeless individual.

The opportunity to talk to the second homeless individual last Saturday came when I joined youth group students from my church participating in volunteer service and evangelism activities for the homeless. The students prepared warm soups and sandwiches for homeless individuals and introduced Christianity to them while serving food. It was the first time that I had participated in the activities.

Towards the end of the activities, there came a time when all volunteers were divided into pairs and handed out the Christian leaflets to the homeless. My partner and I approached a middle-aged, black homeless man sitting on a bench.

I introduced myself to the homeless man and asked to shake his hands. He also gave me his name and held my hands. I did not know what else to say, so I asked where he was born. He said that it was Alexandria. I told him that Alexandria was the first place that I lived after immigrating to the U.S. and that I graduated from T.C. Williams Senior High School. He asked me in which year I graduated. When I told him that it was 1977, he then looked at my face for a moment and said that he graduated from the same high school only a year later in 1978. I told him that my younger sister graduated in 1979. He responded that he had an older sister who graduated in the same year as I. Wow! What a small world! I learned that he was in the orchestra and the choir while in high school.

I cautiously asked him how he had become homeless. He shared with me that he had worked at a supermarket for more than twenty years but lost his job due to severe arthritis in his hip and knees. He applied for disability benefits, but the governmental review process was too slow. He was currently receiving vocational training so that he could hopefully take an office job in the future. I was also inspired to hear that he was directing a choir on a part-time basis at a nearby church. He mentioned that seven of the twelve choir members for their eight o'clock worship service were also homeless. He continued to talk about the songs he had selected for this Sunday's worship.

He shared with me that, during Lent,[49] he had been encouraging the other homeless choir members not to let go of hope. After all, Jesus fasted for forty days in the desert. At that point, I was rendered speechless, so I asked him to pray for me and the student standing beside me. The three of us held hands together and prayed. I originally planned to console the man but was instead it was I that was consoled a great deal by him that day.

When I returned home, I went straight down to the basement to search for his pictures in the high school yearbooks. Yes, there I found pictures of him and his sister. He still had much of the same look from forty years ago. I am thinking about visiting his church soon to hear the singing by the choir that he directs.[50]

49 In Christianity, Lent refers to the period starting from Ash Wednesday until the day before Easter. Excluding the six Sundays, it is forty days.

50 Shortly thereafter, I visited the church early on a Sunday morning with another student from my Sunday school to listen to the praise music by the choir he conducted.

Birth Father And Stepfather

AM 1310
September 8, 2000

The fall soccer season for my two sons kicked off with the start of a new semester. My older son, a seventh grader, and the younger son, a fourth grader, have been playing soccer in a neighborhood league for several years. There is a soccer fever in the Washington, D.C. area such that there may only be a handful of children in my neighborhood who have not played soccer.

This is the first season since the formation of the Burke Athletic Club to which my children belong. As you might have read in a recent Washington Post article, the Burke Soccer Club had enjoyed a near-monopoly status for youth soccer in the Burke area for many years as the only youth league in the area. With around thirteen hundred members, it had been holding two seasons each year—one in the spring and another in the fall.

However, a group of parents decided to form a new soccer league. They were not happy with the existing league's administrative and financial mismanagement. The leader of this group of new parents was a Korean woman. She was a lawyer and happened to be the coach of my older son's team. As a result of her hard work talking to and persuading the other coaches and parents, she was able to help launch a new league under the name of Burke Athletic Club, with more than eleven hundred members.

The existing Burke Soccer Club suffered a devastating reduction in memberships, now only having around three hundred. Unlike the existing club, the new Burke Athletic Club registered itself as a non-profit organization. The new club has also set as its goals to provide more support to members parents, students and coaches. It is doubtful whether the Burke Soccer Club will even be able to hold games for the fall season. The arrogance of being the dominant soccer league in the Burke area for so long that no one would dare to start a new one had brought down this group.

Then I found something interesting while looking at the roster of the players and the parents for my younger son's team. Four names were listed as the parents of one player. I found out later that the parents of the player were divorced and both remarried. Therefore, he now had two sets of parents. What impressed me the most was that while this player was living with his birth mother and stepfather, his team's coach was his stepfather and the assistant coach, none other than the birth father.

I was at first puzzled on how the two fathers could get along with each other so well to volunteer for the same team. To add to that, his birth mother was the team manager in charge of taking care of all different administrative tasks for the team, and she seemed to work well with both fathers. I do not know the reasons for the birth parents' divorce, but they were setting a good example for other divorced couples with children.

Divorced parents must not take actions out of their personal emotions against each other which may, in turn, adversely affect their children. Even if they might have gone through a bad divorce, they should try to make sure that there was no further harm to their children in their upbringing or education. Parents' divorce does not change their relationships with their children. It is, therefore, necessary for the parents to have the maturity to control their emotions for the sake of their children's future.

The two coaches with the players.[51]

51 The one in the middle on the front row is my second son. Interesting that the boys picked "Pansies" as the team's name. U12 refers to the age of 12 and under.

Buchangbusu (夫唱婦隨)

The Korea Times–Washington D.C.
July 4, 2014

Buchangbusu is an idiomatic phrase that the wife (婦) follows when her husband (夫) sings or demands. To be precise, it means that wife is the one following her husband and not the other way around. In a sense, the order of the word, husband and wife, may not be appropriate in a gender-equal society.

I often look at the turnover statistics of teachers in Fairfax County Public Schools. Quite a few female teachers resign due to the move of their husband's job. It seems that there are more such cases in the Washington, D.C. area where the federal government is located. Following the husband's job to a new area would certainly create hardships for a wife having to find a new job, especially if she were pursuing her own career.

In the last week, nevertheless, I heard a story about a husband who changed his job because of his wife's move. He was one of the cluster[52] assistant superintendents in Fairfax County. Each cluster assistant superintendent oversees directing and supervising around twenty-five schools in the Fairfax County Public Schools. I got to know this cluster assistant superintendent well after our visit to Korea together a few years ago. He has, however, resigned from his post to follow his wife who was transferred to another state by her employer.

When a senior administrator retires or resigns, the Fairfax County School Board generally passes a resolution at a regular meeting to honor the administrator and to commend the hard work

---

52 There used to be eight clusters in Fairfax County at the time. The eight clusters later became restructured to five regions.

and contributions they made to the school system. The family members and other friends of the honoree are also invited to the meeting. Along with adoption of the resolution, gifts are presented, commemorative photos are taken, and individual board members make remarks. The administrator is also given an opportunity to say their farewells. The whole event is broadcast live on the school system's cable TV channel.

As I was leaving the meeting where the resolution was presented, I heard that the cluster assistant superintendent's wife cried. She had been already feeling sorry deep in her heart about her husband having to move to a different part of the country. However, her feelings grew even bigger when she heard congratulatory words and good wishes from the school board members and the superintendent. The realization of what her husband's presence meant for the Fairfax County school system hit her hard.

It was the second time that this cluster assistant superintendent was changing his job because of his wife's move. The first time happened fourteen years ago. He was working as a principal at a school in another state at the time but moved to Fairfax County to follow his wife's job transfer to Fairfax County. It was not easy for him to find a principal's job in a place where he had no connection at all. Therefore, he applied for a lower assistant principal position. He managed to secure one after many interviews at several schools. He later transferred to a high school assistant principal's position before becoming a high school principal. He then became a cluster assistant superintendent, a position considered to be part of the superintendent's leadership team, with the responsibility for around twenty-five schools.

Now, he is leaving Fairfax County to take on a new job as the principal of a middle school in the state of his wife's new workplace. He is sacrificing again for his wife. He is an outstanding educator and a manager with much to offer. I believe that it will not be long before he takes on a more important role in his new school district, but I realize there is no guarantee for that.

Regardless, his love for his wife, leaving behind his career growth twice, is certainly something that we all need to echo.

A similar case was with Dr. Karen Garza, the first female superintendent of the Fairfax County Public Schools. Her husband gave up his job and followed her from Texas last year. Her husband had to stay home for a year until he could land a job. One of my neighbors, a lawyer who lived right next door to our house, too, stayed home for three years to do housework and to look after their school-aged children when his wife wanted to return to her work. It is something men do not usually think about. These are all good examples for us to learn from.

The question on the order of "husband and wife" is still on my mind.

Enjoying oysters with Mr. James Kacur[53]
on a cruise while visiting Korea in 2010.

53 Mr. James Kacur was a high school principal at the time and later became an assistant superintendent. On an invitation from the Office of Education of South Gyeongnam Province, Korea, he made a presentation to principals.

Enemy And Ally

The Korea Times-Washington D.C.
December 15, 2011
September 13, 2019

About a couple of months ago, I received a campaign contribution check for the school board election in November this year.[54] The donor knew well that I had failed to secure the endorsement from the Fairfax County Democratic Committee. However, she was still recommending me to run.

I had kept the check until recently before returning it to her as I had decided to formally submit a request for withdrawing my candidacy for the school board election. The donor was none other than Tessie Wilson, a rival Republican candidate against whom I had first run as a Democrat for the Braddock District seat on the school board in 1995.

There were three candidates in my 1995 election. I upended everyone's expectation and was elected with fifty-one percent of the votes. The result must have been a shock to Tessie Wilson. She had a lot of experience in elections and politics as an officer of the Fairfax County Republican Committee. Besides, she had much more knowledge on educational issues, whereas I was a novice with no experience.

A local newspaper included the above illustration to describe

54 The year is 2019.

the campaign between her and me in that year's election. It was, somehow, that fierce. In their view, the battle between us looked like a physical fight grabbing each other's necks and shaking fists. Anyway, after losing the election, Tessie Wilson made a thorough preparation for the next election to be held in four years later and won the return match against me in 1999. I was not vigilant enough in that election and my opponent had caught me off guard.

I had a chance to come back in 2003 after failing the reelection. This time, I ran for an at-large seat representing the entire Fairfax County rather than the Braddock District alone. Whether an at-large member or a district member, each school board member has one vote at the school board meetings. The difference is that the district members tend to pay closer attention to the issues affecting their respective districts while the at-large members focus on countywide issues. I found that dealing with countywide issues was more attractive, so I felt that there was no need to run against Ms. Wilson again. In that year's election, both of us were elected together. We repeated the same in 2007. Thus, we had been able to work together as colleagues for eight years.

However, even after winning the elections together, our relationship had not been always smooth. I guess the experience of each of us losing once to each other must have made it awkward for both of us. We also had honest differences on various policy issues simply due to our differences in educational philosophy and political belief. Nevertheless, Ms. Wilson's passion, dedication, commitment, and service towards the education earned my respect.

She also paid special attention to special education issues and college education funding. For once, we were in opposition, having to beat the other as an opponent, but our relationship had grown to appreciate and respect each other's commitment to public education through the eight years of working together side by side as colleagues. She once whispered into my ear that she and her husband, both strong Republicans, voted for me, a Democrat, in the 2011 election.

Our relationship became friendlier after Ms. Wilson's

retirement at the end of 2011. The 2011 election brought in six new members to the board—that was half of the board. All the newly elected board members eagerly wanted to play important roles in policymaking and budgeting with great ambitions of their own. However, reality did not always allow them to realize their beliefs or pursuits.

As candidates, you could make many admirable promises during the campaign, but once you were elected, you would need to see the bigger picture and consider the views of other board members as well. The board members are often forced to make political compromises and concessions because some of their fellow board members may have completely different ideas of their own. Nevertheless, I saw quite often some highly motivated new members making unreasonable demands. Whenever I had to deal with such situations, the absence of the former, more experienced colleagues was felt more deeply just like an old proverb, "you don't know what you've got until you have lost it."

The appearance of the many first-time elected members was a crucial turning point for me and Ms. Wilson to see each other from new perspectives. And our relationship became closer and stronger as we began helping and encouraging each other. That is how she, still a Republican, came to feel sorry for my failure to get an official endorsement from the Fairfax County Democratic Committee and to give me a campaign donation, encouraging me to continue running for the election.

That "there is no eternal enemy or ally" seems to be true. Of course, I do not want any of my allies to turn into an enemy. But, at the same time, I should leave enough space in my heart for an enemy to become my ally. I should never automatically assume that an enemy would remain as an enemy forever.

Political Disagreement And Human Relationship

The Korea Times-Washington D.C.
March 14, 2014

I saw Mr. Robert Dix and Mr. Patrick Mullins at a high school basketball game two weeks ago. Both are die-hard Republicans. On the contrary, I am a loyal Democrat, so it is not always comfortable meeting with them. However, if you put aside the politics, I can recognize that they are good people. If I cannot handle myself well in interacting with them because of our political differences, it is then something that I must try hard to improve upon.

I first got to know them in 1995 when I ran for the first school board election. At that time, Mr. Dix was the supervisor for the Hunter Mill District in Fairfax County. I was feeling desperate at the time because I did not have anything to show to the voters as a candidate. That was why I put in extra efforts to seek a stop-gap appointment for six months for an at-large seat on the school board.

The stop-gap appointments for several seats were needed to be made at the time as the school board was changing from an appointed to an elected board. Prior to the school board switching to an elected board, the school board members in Fairfax County used to be appointed by the Fairfax County Board of Supervisors. The three at-large seats on the school board used to be nominated by the chairman of the Board of Supervisors and then voted on by the Board of Supervisors.

There were ten supervisors, including the chairman, but they were equally divided between the Republicans and the Democrats at the time. My nomination was put forth by the Democratic chairman Kate Hanley several times, but it was repeatedly rejected by the Board of Supervisors on a tie vote of five to five. Eventually, my nomination passed after a political compromise under which the five Democratic supervisors would give up one at-large appointment the Republicans. Nevertheless, Mr. Dix still opposed my appointment. He was the lone dissenter.

I received a phone call from Mr. Dix's chief of staff on the morning after the vote confirming my appointment. The chief of staff relayed to me a request from Mr. Dix to have a lunch with me. I flatly refused it. I was upset. I received a call again the next day, but my reaction was still the same.

Mr. Mullins has been the chairman of the Republican Party of Virginia since 2009.[55] He is considered a political mogul in Virginia. However, he was serving as the chairman of the Fairfax County Republican Committee (FCRC) at the time I ran for the school board for the first time in 1995. Obviously, as the chairman of the FCRC, he was responsible for helping all Republican candidates in Fairfax County to win in that year's election. Therefore, it is not exaggeration to label him as the top decision maker and the strategist to come up with plans to defeat me.

As the first Asian candidate and an opponent of an FCRC officer at that time, I certainly felt that the Republicans were resorting to many underhanded tactics against me. Rumors were being spread to link me to the Unification Church, based on my last name being Moon and me being a Korean, and that I was receiving the full support of the Moonies.[56]

So, my relationships with Mr. Dix and Mr. Mullins started unpleasantly. However, as time passed, I began seeing the human sides of the two, and my perspectives on them began changing as well. Despite his busy schedule as a supervisor, Mr. Dix continued

---

55 Mr. Mullins resigned from the chairmanship of the Republican Party of Virginia on January 31, 2015. Sadly, he passed away at the age of seventy-nine in a car accident in May 2017.

56 Followers of the Reverend Sun Myung Moon, the founder of the Unification Church, were often derogatively called the Moonies.

volunteering as a coach for a neighborhood basketball team for high school students. He also suffered a loss in the 1999 election just like me. Perhaps because we were in the same boat of a defeat, I could empathize with his pain. No words were needed. However, he had kept his chin up and did not stop teaching basketball to students. We also often saw each other in high school basketball games.

Mr. Mullins is a founding member and a former president of the Annandale Rotary Club that I joined in 1998. He moved to another area in the state by the time I joined the club, so we did not have a chance to work together in the same club, though. He also served as the Governor of Rotary District 7610, to which my club belonged, for two years from the year 2000.

He once asked me for one of my campaign signs during the 2011 election. He told me that his grandson living near Richmond, the capital city of Virginia, had seen my campaign sign when he had visited him in Fairfax and wanted to get one so that he could put it in front yard of his house. I gladly gave him a sign. He shared with me afterwards that the people used to ask who I was when they saw my sign in front of his grandson's house.

When I saw Mr. Mullins again two weeks ago at the basketball game, he introduced his daughter to me. She was a teacher at a high school in Fairfax County. His daughter said that she had seen me from a distance at her school event just the day before. She looked at me and her father alternately and then asked whether we were in good terms. I responded with an awkward smile.

I keep reminding myself that political differences should not damage pure human relationships.

With Mr. Patrick Mullins and his granddaughter,
a high school volleyball player, after a game (2017)

Attorneys And Teachers

The Korea Times-Washington D.C.
Updated: March 2019

Last week, I attended a meeting of the Asian Educators Association, an association for Asian teachers and other staff members within Fairfax County Public Schools (FCPS).

This organization was formed around seven to eight years ago and currently has approximately sixty members. Although its membership size may be small now, it aims to promote camaraderie and information sharing among its members and to help them develop leadership skills. I hope that this organization will continue to grow to play a big part in the education of the students and become beneficial to the local community as well.

In that meeting, there was some time allocated for a dialogue with Dr. Karen Garza, the superintendent of FCPS who had been newly appointed on July 1. An opportunity for teachers and staff members to meet with the superintendent in person does not happen every day, so I could see palpable excitement in the air.

There was also time for the attendees to go around and briefly introduce themselves. One principal shared that he had originally thought of going into the legal profession per his parents' wish. He then later changed the course to become an educator instead. Listening to that, I remembered some other people who used to work as attorneys but changed their careers to education. It would not be an easy decision to go from an attorney to a schoolteacher unless at a college level. Then again, an extraordinary passion for teaching could make it possible.

Pat Hynes, my colleague on the school board, is one such case. She represents the Hunter Mill District in Fairfax County. She used to work as an attorney for a large law firm in New York but quit her job, as she wanted to take care of her young children after getting married. Once the children had reached certain ages, she returned to work, not as an attorney this time but instead as an elementary school teacher. She had taught at a Fairfax County school for around ten years before getting elected to the school board in 2011.

Once elected, she had no choice but to quit her job as a teacher in Fairfax County due to a rule prohibiting a school board member being employed in the same school district. However, she just could not give up teaching, so she is currently working as an instructional assistant in a nearby school district.[57]

With Ms. Patricia Hynes, a school board colleague

57 Ms. Pat Hynes now teaches fulltime in an elementary school as a regular teacher after retiring from the school board with me in 2019.

She is now working as a full-time teacher there because she feels that she will not have enough time to adequately fulfill her responsibilities for her students as a full-time teacher while managing the work as a school board member.

One of my children's favorite teachers when they werc in the elementary school used to be an attorney, too. He had originally worked as a teacher before becoming an attorney. He then returned to teaching after a few years of law practice. He felt that there was nothing more rewarding than educating students. Around ten years ago, he was selected as a recipient of the Milken Educator Awards given to the best teachers in the U.S. He enjoyed applying his law-school-trained, Socratic method to his classes.

Mr. George Weiner, a Milliken Award winner

My next-door neighbor also retired from his law practice in early forties and now teaches U.S. Government in a high school in Fairfax County. The course curriculum contains many parts related to law, so it is suitable for a lawyer to teach. He is highly respected in his school. Someone that I have known since my law school days teaches in Fairfax County, too. She used to work for a large law firm in New York at first and then for a mid-size firm in Washington, D.C. She was apparently not satisfied with her legal work, so she changed her job to teaching history in high school. One of my church members recently retired from the law practice at the age of sixty to teach in a high school.

A former neighbor of mine Mr. Gregory Walsh at a graduation

With Mr. James Insun We at Centreville High School
—he teaches there after retiring from law practice (2019)

Dr. Sloan Presidio, who is the assistant superintendent for instructional services in charge of the general education in the Fairfax County Public Schools, is a similar case, too. He started his career as a teacher and enrolled in a law school while teaching. After becoming an attorney, he had worked at a large law firm in Washington, D.C. for a few years, but eventually returned to teaching as he could not forget his first love for education.

His high competence is well acknowledged by everyone around, and I have no doubt that it is just a matter of time we would see him as a superintendent somewhere.[58] If he wanted, he could become a superintendent even now, but I understand that he wants his young children to get good education in Fairfax County for now.

I also thought about teaching, so I asked around. I have heard that I could perhaps teach U.S. Government or ESOL (English for Speakers of Other Languages). I will not be able to teach and be a school board member at the same time in Fairfax County, but it is possible for me to teach in a different district. I am also glad to hear that there are people willing to write recommendation letters for me if I wanted to go that direction. I sometimes feel very much tempted to put these thoughts into action.

---

58 As of May 2021, he is the Chief Academic Officer of Fairfax County Public Schools, in charge of both general education and special education.

With Dr. Sloan Presidio at my retirement reception (2019)

Racial Prejudice And Discrimination

Washington Media
October 27, 1999

It was a few years ago[59] when my church choir members were on their way back to the church after attending an anniversary service at a sister church. The sister church was located around three hours away by car. We rented a charter bus as the number of choir members was large. The choir members enjoyed having plenty of time to talk to each other on the bus and participated in some fun group activities on the way back after the worship service.

I was the emcee that day. I tried to make the activities as fun as possible and encourage everyone to fully participate. I felt grateful that the choir members followed my directions, though silly at times, without much complaint. I provided the relatively new members with opportunities to introduce themselves and set aside time to sing old songs together. Of course, I added some comical stories here and there lest should they get bored during the three-hour bus trip.

Then, when the bus had almost reached our church, something completely unexpected happened. One of the choir members came forward to make some funny jokes. He included a joke about the O.J. Simpson murder trial[60] that had just ended at that time. I

---

59 1995

60 O.J. Simpson, a black, former professional football superstar, was charged in June 1994 of murdering his former wife and her boyfriend, both of whom were white. In the jury trial that ended in October 1995, he was found not guilty. The trial was known to have many racial implications.

cannot remember the exact content of the joke, but we laughed a lot.

The bus driver then threw a question which I found difficult to comprehend at first. It was more of a protest than a question. He asked whether we were true Christians. I did not understand what his true intention was. As the emcee, I answered the question with an "of course." The driver then threw another question which immediately quieted the bus, and I also became cautious in answering.

He asked, "how could you be so racially prejudiced when you declared to be a Christian?" The driver was able to figure out the joke about O.J. Simpson because there were enough English words included. To the black driver, a joke about another black person sounded like an insult to all black people. I repeatedly explained to him that the joke was not made with racial prejudice. However, he did not seem to be convinced.

I have heard a lot about racial prejudice and discrimination in my fifteen years of law practice and during the past four years as a school board member. There have been quite a few people who would hastily assume racism whenever they felt to have been unfairly treated by someone from a different racial background.

There are many Koreans doing business in Washington, D.C., who claim to have been unfairly accused as being racist by their black customers. Customers sometimes assume that they were being treated unfairly because they were black, even when the business owners were only reacting to their misbehaviors and not their racial background.

The same possibility of similar misinterpretation or unfair accusation, however, exists amongst Koreans, too. Not all unfair treatments that we may have received should be automatically considered as racial discrimination. Interactions among the people of different racial backgrounds should not automatically trigger people to see things with a racial lens.

It was never due to racial prejudice or discrimination that the church choir members burst into laughter while listening to a joke about O.J. Simpson on the bus. However, it is also true that no one thought about how the black bus driver could interpret it at the time either. Racial prejudice and discrimination: these are not the words we should throw around indiscriminately, but we should never practice or tolerate them. At the same time, we should always be mindful of situations that may lead to a misunderstanding.

Chapter 6

People I Have Met

Introduction

Humans are social animals by nature; thus, we cannot avoid the draw to meet and interact with other people. Some of them will leave good memories, while some others will not. Some might be helpful, and some might only inflict wounds. Some we would like to see again; some others we might not even want to think about.

We make good first impressions and help people, perhaps even becoming someone whom they would want to see again; however, on the other hand, the exact opposite could be the case. We might have honestly done our best, but our best efforts might still be insufficient to some people—or our good intentions might even be misconstrued.

If we were to live an entirely solitary existence, we would not have to worry about these things; however, we have no choice but to live in relationships with others from birth to death. If we want to make even a little positive influence in our relationships with others, we should train ourselves to look at things from the other person's position. I am not saying that such training requires you to ignore your own needs, but it can help to make you a more generous human being.

During the sixty plus years of my life, I have met a lot of people. In particular, the last twenty-five years of public service in the U.S. has provided me with the opportunities to meet people with diverse backgrounds. I thank everyone who has helped me. I love everyone who has loved me. They have made me who I am today.

On the other hand, I want to have a loving heart even for those who have not been helpful to me, or even disliked me. I have truly felt hurt at times because of them. However, I am sure I have not always had a heart to help them or like them, either. They must also have been hurt from time to time because of me. I am sorry for that, and I pray for their forgiveness.

No one is perfect. I am far from being perfect myself. Nevertheless, there are people who care for me. It is incumbent upon me to do the same for others despite their flaws.

Kate Hanley

The Korea Times-Washington D.C.
April 26, 2013

I attended an annual award ceremony sponsored by the Fairfax County Federation of Citizens Associations (FCFCA) about three weeks ago. This event is in its sixty-third year. The FCFCA is a voluntary federation of homeowners, condominiums, and civic associations in Fairfax County. Not all such associations in the county are members; nevertheless, it represents around one hundred twenty thousand households, roughly thirty percent of all households in the county.

The FCFCA is a nonpartisan organization. Its main mission is to collect and convey to the policymakers the opinions of county residents on various issues which directly affect their daily lives. It publishes its official positions on the county's budget, education, transportation, environment, legislation, and social services, engaging in lobbying activities to achieve its published positions. In addition, each year, it selects and awards county residents who have made significant contributions in various fields.

Among the recipients of the awards this year were several individuals with whom I have close, personal relationships. Peter Murphy won the Citizen of the Year Award. He has served on the Fairfax County Planning Commission for over thirty years with twenty-four years as its chairman. The Fairfax County Planning Commission is responsible for reviewing zoning and other land use applications within the county.

The recipients for the Citation of Merit Award were Rose Chu and Phyllis Payne. Rose Chu had served on the Health Care Advisory Board for more than twenty-five years, and Phyllis Payne is a prominent advocate for later school start times.

However, Kate Hanley caught my greatest attention—she received the Lifetime Achievement Award. She has been considered the "Godmother" of the Fairfax County Democratic Committee. She built her significant political influence over the course of her decades in public service. She began her public service as an appointed school board member representing the Providence District in 1984. She was then elected to become the county supervisor for the same district in a special election held in 1986 and held that position until she was elected as Chairman of the Board of Supervisors in another special election in 1995. After serving as the Chairman until 2003, she retired from county politics. She then served as the Secretary of the Commonwealth of Virginia during Governor Tim Kaine's administration for four years starting in 2006.

I do not recollect exactly when I first got to know her, but I do clearly remember the first time I visited her in her office. It was in the spring of 1995, soon after she had been elected as the Chairman of the Board of Supervisors. At the time, I was preparing to run for my first school board election in November of the same year. I was in desperate need of help, as I had little knowledge about elections and the county's education issues. At the time, I had almost no name recognition in the community, either. As the Fairfax County School Board was in the process of transitioning to an elected board from an appointed one, the Fairfax County Board of Supervisors needed to make stop-gap appointments for two at-large positions on the school board for a six-month period.

As a candidate running in my first school board election, I had nothing to show on my resume other than a strong commitment to serve. Therefore, I thought that a stopgap appointment even just for six months would be quite helpful for my campaign. That way, by the time the election rolled around, I would be seen as an incumbent rather than a brand new kid on the block. So, I went to see Chairman Hanley because she had the power to nominate the candidates for the at-large seats.

In my meeting with her, I explained my plans to run for the

election and asked for a nomination for an at-large seat. I must have put her in an awkward position, but then, perhaps recognizing my resolve, she advised me to closely follow her instructions. She told me to go and ask my supporters to send recommendation letters to all supervisors representing each district in the county. In addition, she urged me to secure supporters to speak on my behalf at the meeting of the Board of Supervisors at which the appointments would be voted on.

At my swearing-in ceremony as an appointed school board member —Ms. Kate Hanley, Chairman of Fairfax County Board of Supervisors, is in the middle (June 1995).

Following her advice, I prepared sample recommendation letters and envelopes for my supporters to use and asked them to send their letters to all ten supervisors in the county. The supervisors must have been surprised to receive dozens of letters each. I also recruited a couple of law school friends –who lived in Fairfax County, one who was a prosecutor and another who worked in private practice, along with some of the leaders in the local Korean community to speak at the Board of Supervisors meeting. After multiple rounds of voting and political compromises, my nomination for appointment was approved, and I eventually won the November election as well.

An occasion for which I am even more grateful came after I failed in my re-election bid for the school board in 1999. I felt embarrassed and was quite discouraged by the loss. Chairman Hanley then appointed me to an at-large position on the Fairfax County Planning Commission. I had no prior land use experience for the appointment, but Chairman Hanley wanted to encourage me to stay in public service. She might not have wanted to see the first Asian-American to be elected to public office in Virginia to disappear in disillusionment.

Her encouragement worked. Four years later in 2003, I ran for the school board again and won. Since then, I have been elected two more times and am now in my fourth term as a school board member. Kate Hanley has been a life saver and a mentor for me in every political crisis.

Congratulating her for the well-deserved award three weeks ago, I could feel a strong desire in my own heart to be remembered by people out there as a person who helped and guided them, just as Kate Hanley had done for me. I began asking myself about how I might go about achieving just that.

Janie Strauss

AM 1310
August 24, 2000

I recently read an article in a Korean newspaper that the Korean government was likely to abolish its quota system for the adoption of Korean children by families overseas. It was reported that a number of larger countries, including the U.S., were demanding that the Korean government quickly ratify the Convention on Protection of Children and Co-operation in Respect of Intercountry Adoption passed at the Thirty-third Hague Conference on Private International Law held in 1993. This convention stipulated the right to the expeditious domestic and international adoption of the children in need of protection.

The newspaper article reported that the ratification by the Korean government would lift the limitation on the number of overseas adoptions and would likewise increase the number of the Korean children being adopted by families in the U.S. The number of the Korean children adopted since 1958 has reached 143,388 for the overseas adoptions and 57,945 for domestic. It is said that 2,409 children were adopted abroad in the past year alone.

It is possible that Korea might acquire a stigma of being an orphan exporter if the adoption quota were abolished. On the other hand, we have the responsibility to help the children find new parents quickly if we truly consider the needs of these young children to grow up in a nurturing environment.

I would like to share the adoption stories of Janie Strauss,[61]

---

61 Ms. Strauss retired from the school board at the same time with me in December 2019. She had been the longest serving school board member, having served for twenty-four years, ever since Fairfax County began electing its school board members.

a school board member in Fairfax County. Janie Strauss and her husband had hoped for a large family; however, their second child did not come along for a long time after the birth of their first daughter, so they decided to adopt a child in the meantime. Once it became apparent that finding a child for adoption in the U.S. was not easy, they turned to foreign countries.

After going through many ups and downs in the process, they finally adopted a girl from South America. They felt that one adoption was not enough, so they decided to adopt one more, a boy this time. Their efforts to adopt a boy eventually led them to Korea. They had found a child to be adopted, and the whole process had been completed.

Then, they found out that the child was in poor health. The Korean adoption agency advised them that they did not have to take the sick child and offered to find them a new healthy child instead. The couple immediately rejected the agency's offer—they believed that any child, even one who was sick, deserved a chance to live a full life. They were advised that the child they would adopt was in a such critical condition that there was a chance that he might die in the airplane before even arriving in the U.S. or that he might not live a normal life even if he survived the journey. Janie and her husband, Bill, however, thought that it was their mission and prayed to God that he would stay alive until he arrived at the hospital in the U.S.

Fortunately, the child survived and is now in high school. He is still able to lead an entirely normal life despite the illness suffered at that time. How could we comprehend the idea of adopting a sick child knowing that it would be difficult for him to live a normal life and of having to deal with enormous medical expenses when the child was not your own?

Some people might think that they were intoxicated with heroism, but that was not the case for the Strausses. Moreover, what would it matter so long as they raised the child with all their heart, even if their action had been just for self-gratification?

Then again, Koreans generally do not seem to look favorably

on adoption. Is that because blood ties are traditionally valued? Or are they just less compassionate than Americans? If not, are we then not yet disciplined enough to put love into practice even though we may seemingly be empathizing while watching sad scenes in the dramas or reading tragic stories in newspapers?

I am hoping for an increase in the rate of adoption of Korean children inside Korea in the future. I also hope to see soon the day when a large portion of the Korean children adopted to the U.S. goes to Korean American families.

With Dranesville School Board member Janie Strauss
and At-Large School Board member Ryan McElveen.
All three of us retired at the end of 2019.

Mark Emery

The Korea Times-Washington D.C.
August 17, 2012

Dr. Mark Emery was one of the two recipients of the Robert Spillane Leadership Award presented by the Fairfax County School Board last week. This award is given out once a year to staff members for their outstanding leadership in honor of Dr. Spillane, who retired in 1998 after serving for twelve years as the superintendent of Fairfax County Public Schools (FCPS).

I first met Dr. Emery in the spring of 1995. I was preparing to run for my first school board election in Fairfax County at the time. Legally speaking, school board elections are supposed to be nonpartisan. However, as political parties are permitted to endorse and provide financial and logistical support to candidates, there is virtually no difference from any other partisan election.

As I did not know how to run for election but considered myself to be a Democrat, I decided to seek an endorsement from the Fairfax County Democratic Committee (FCDC) even though I was not an official member. The FCDC was only planning to endorse three candidates for at-large school board seats, as there were only three at-large seats. Of course, the number of at-large candidates seeking endorsements far exceeded three.

Unfortunately, I failed to secure an endorsement. The three candidates who received the endorsements included a black candidate who had already served on the school board as an appointed member for a long time and a Latina candidate who had been an active member of the FCDC for many years.

For the last spot, I was told later that I was in a close competition with a white male candidate. Although I brought a fresh face to the table, my biggest weak point was my lack of experience in dealing with education issues. On the other hand, the white candidate had been active as an officer in the PTAs of his children's schools for many years. He had also served on the Superintendent Advisory Council for several years. So, in the end, this white candidate was chosen as the third endorsee by the FCDC.

Despite this setback, and after some other ups and downs, I was able to obtain the support from the Braddock District Democratic Committee to run for the Braddock District seat and was elected along with the white candidate who ran for an at-large seat. This man was none other than Dr. Emery.

Dr. Emery was about fifteen years older than me and held a Ph.D. in physics. He worked as a researcher at the Naval Research Laboratory. During the first two years of his term, he had served as the vice chairman of the school board. He then served as its chairman in his third year, demonstrating excellent leadership. However, surprisingly, he lost in his re-election bid in 1999.

After leaving the board, his passion for youth continued, and he ended up playing a critical role in the youth organization called the Fairfax Partnership for Youth—an organization established by the FCPS and leaders in the community who deeply cared about potentially at-risk students in Fairfax County. After retiring from the Naval Research Laboratory with twenty-five years of service, Dr. Emery then became a mid-level manager of the after-school program for middle school students which FCPS launched with financial support from the county government.

As a mid-level manager working for FCPS, Dr. Emery became a subordinate to many of the very same senior staff who used to report to him when he was a board member. Nevertheless, he did not care about where his position stood in the hierarchy. What he had found to be more important was to do the things into which he could pour his passion. He did not feel uncomfortable with the fact that those who used to be under him were now his superiors and that he had to work for people much younger.

He did not necessarily need more income, either, as his wife was a medical doctor, and he was collecting pension benefits. He just wanted to devote the rest of his life to helping students who might not be using their time constructively or might be engaging in undesirable activities. Stares from others or losing his face were not as important to him. He was simply grateful for each student that would be transformed with his help. So, it was no surprise that he received the leadership award last week.

Watching Dr. Emery standing at the awards ceremony, I asked myself whether I could be like him. Honestly, I was not so sure. I may not have the courage to do things while losing face no matter how passionate I am about the work and however rewarding the work may be. I am fully aware that I will not stay as a school board member forever and that elected officials are elected to serve the community; however, it is still unlikely for my pride to allow me to do so.

My head seems to discern what is more important, but my heart does not seem to follow it. Perhaps I will ask myself again whether I would get better as I become older.

With Dr. Mark Emery on the far left in the back
at a middle school event (1999)

All wearing Dr. Seuss' hats at a school board meeting to emphasize
importance of reading—Dr. Mark Emery is the 7th from the left (1998)

Young Sil Lee And Hye Kyung Hahn

AM 1310
September 29, 2000

Young Sil Lee (a/k/a Young Sil Park), a senior deaconess of the Korean United Methodist Church of Greater Washington, which I attend, was called to be with God at the dawn on September 24. She was born in Pyongyang in August 1905, so she had lived for ninety-five years before passing way. While I am sure that her family was sad, I hope that her long, fulfilling life could be a consolation.

She graduated from Soongui Girls' High School and then studied childcare at Ewha Womans College, now known as Ewha Womans University. She married the Elder Kyung Ho Park in 1926. As far as I know, the Elder Park was the first person to teach piano in college in Korea. The deaconess had served the Lord as an alto in the church choir and devoted herself in serving others since immigrating to the U.S. in 1954. Her cooking skills were well recognized, with her dumplings and naengmyeon (cold noodles) being particularly famous. She eagerly invited pastors visiting the Washington, D.C. area to stay at her home, even if for one night.

She was a traditional Korean beauty and was good at English. She never neglected to maintain good relationships with the people around her. I did not have as much of a chance to have a close personal relationship with her, although I often talked with her third son, Elder Choong Hyun Park, a pathologist at the Fairfax Hospital—the large age gap between me and her might have prevented me from having a closer interaction with her.

Even so, she had given me an unforgettable gift around five years ago. It was in October 1995, when I was running for the school board for the first time and frantically campaigning. All candidates become desperate to raise money during campaign season, and, to my surprise, I received an unexpected donation from her. She was ninety years old at the time and did not have any income; however, she sent me twenty dollars.

I had quite a few donors, with some of them making large donations. Nevertheless, her twenty dollars gave me more strength than anyone else's donation. There are supporters who want to send me campaign contributions but give up because they feel that the amounts are too small. However, for candidates, no donation is too small. On the contrary, candidates often see the warm hearts of their supporters in those small gifts, and those small donations are great encouragements. Her gift will be remembered for life as one of most unforgettable donations for me.

The words of Hye Kyung Hahn (a/k/a Alice Hahn Kim), another senior deaconess, who gave a eulogy at the Deaconess Young Sil Lee's farewell service, are still ringing in my heart. Deaconess Hahn used to call the deceased Deaconess Lee as an older sister and is the wife of the late the Rev. Jacob Siung Duk Kim. The Rev. Kim had served our church as a co-pastor with the Rev. Andrew Chai Kyung Whang for many years. She turned ninety this year.

In commemorating the deceased Deaconess Lee, she confessed her feelings that she could be the next one to pass as she was witnessing the older people around her leaving this world. Deaconess Hahn's own husband left her to meet God a few years ago. As she was bidding farewell to Deaconess Lee with much regret, she then asked Deaconess Lee to go tell her husband and the Rev. Whang and his wife to wait for her as she would join them shortly. My heart sobbed with the thoughts of how difficult the past years must have been for her without her husband.

The empty hearts of the elderly around us, especially the elderly living alone after losing their spouses, would be beyond our ability to comprehend. That farewell service reminded me of our needs to put in more efforts to find ways to fill those empty hearts.

Dr. William Dunkum

It was during my high school senior year in the U.S. The seniors voted to select the superlatives among themselves each year. For each category, two students were selected—one male and one female student. The categories included "most likely to succeed", "best-dressed", "most popular", etc. It was an honor to be selected because it meant being recognized by your classmates.

I had never imagined to be selected for anything, but my classmates voted for me to be one of the Most Intellectual students. My female counterpart selected was none other than the student with the highest GPA in my school at the time. She was the only student who graduated with all As for the entire four years of high school career. Unlike these days, it was rare to get all As for four years back when I was in high school.

I learned later that my selection had even gone into the second round of voting. Three male students had actually tied with the most votes in the first round. Then, somehow, votes came in droves for me in the second round. Both of my competitors were good friends of mine, one entering Harvard with me and the other going to MIT. The female student enrolled at Princeton and majored in chemistry. She is currently a professor of chemical engineering at UC Berkeley.

The selected superlatives all had to have their pictures taken for the school newspaper. We chose the chemistry lab for the picture. We put on a lab gown and goggles but then thought that we would not be easily recognized with goggles on. In the end, we decided to put our goggles overhead. Our picture was published in the school newspaper.

It was the day that the newspaper came out. I was taking an organic chemistry class at the time and saw a photo on the door of the chemistry lab. It was the clip of our picture from the school newspaper. But there was a comment written in red ink at the bottom of the picture, "SO WHY ARE THEY SO DUMB ABOUT GOGGLES?"

I quickly removed it. I found out later that it was done by Dr. William Dunkum, the head of the science department. He was pointing out our failure to follow the safety rules in the chemistry lab by the supposedly two smartest students in the school.

Dr. Dunkum had always been kind to me. He helped me go to the Governor's School after my junior year and selected me to receive the Math & Science Award from Rensselaer Polytechnic Institute that eventually led me to even dream of applying to Harvard in the first place. He wrote me excellent recommendation letters when I applied for college. Yet he also did not hesitate to point out my mistakes.

Dr. Dunkum could have taught on a college level with his doctoral degree in physics, but he purposely chose to teach in high school. I took his physics class during my junior year. Under his outstanding leadership as the head of the science department, our school's science program improved a great deal and was among the best of any school in the area. In my senior year, an organic chemistry class was offered to students for the first time at my school, which was rare for high schools at the time. He was also a bit of a Renaissance man. To celebrate Newton's birthday, he played classical music during physics class on a piano he borrowed from the music department.

My dear teacher, unfortunately, suffered from hemophilia. He taught at my school for a few more years after I graduated. He passed away at a young age while travelling around the world. He was too good to have passed away so early.

I still cherish that photo clip he had posted on door to the chemistry lab.

Gerry Hyland And Earl Flanagan

The Korea Times-Washington D.C.
February 9, 2018

Last Saturday was quite a busy day for me. I volunteered to package food at Colvin Run Elementary School in Fairfax County. The seven schools within the Langley Pyramid[62] in the Fairfax County public school system had purchased around one hundred thousand meals equivalent of food with funds they raised. In the evening, I also had to attend a reception sponsored by the Fairfax Symphony Orchestra to recognize some of the best orchestral students in Fairfax County. After that, I stopped by a charity fundraising event sponsored by the Rotary Club of Vienna.

Still, I was fortunate to be able to relax a bit by playing baduk (Go) during the day at a gathering of baduk hobbyists that meets once every two or three months. However, the earliest event I attended that day was the Mount Vernon District Town Hall meeting. Some of the remarks that I heard at that meeting impressed me very much.

The Mount Vernon District is one of the nine magisterial districts within Fairfax County. The residents of each district elect a supervisor to represent them on the Board of Supervisors of

62 In the Fairfax County public school system, a pyramid refers to a group of schools with one high school at the vertex and the other feeder schools below. Generally, a pyramid consists of one high school, one middle school, and six to eight elementary schools. The schools in the same pyramid maintain organic relationship with each other and engage in activities such as information exchange, joint staff development, grade-level goal-setting, etc.

Fairfax County. The district town hall meetings are organized by the district supervisors, and it was the thirty-first annual meeting for the Mount Vernon District.

The Mount Vernon District Town Hall meeting was first started by the former supervisor Gerry Hyland. He served as a supervisor for twenty-eight years from 1988 and retired at the end of 2015. He had led the meeting every year for the twenty-eight years that he had held the office. The current supervisor is continuing in the tradition.

From the left: the current Mount Vernon Supervisor Daniel Storck; former Mount Vernon Supervisor Gerry Hyland; and the former planning commissioner Earl Flannagan

That day, there was some time set aside to thank the Mount Vernon District Planning Commissioner, Earl Flanagan, who was retiring at the end of March this year. For Fairfax County, traditionally, the supervisors appoint the planning commissioners. The planning commission makes preliminary decisions on whether to approve or disapprove various development applications in the county and planning commissioners play important roles within their district.

Mr. Flanagan has been serving on the planning commission since his appointment by former Mount Vernon District Supervisor Hyland in 2007. One of the most surprising facts that I learned that day was that he was ninety-three years old. In other words, he was already over eighty when he had first been appointed as a planning commissioner. It is rare for someone over the age of eighty to be appointed to a public office or to accept such an appointment.

Even more surprising fact was that he and the former supervisor Mr. Hyland ran against each other in the supervisor election held in 1991. At the time, Mr. Hyland was running for re-election for another four years as the Democratic candidate, and Mr. Flanagan was the Republican candidate challenging Mr. Hyland. Mr. Hyland was successful in re-election and ended up serving for seven terms in total.

After that, Mr. Flanagan had another unsuccessful campaign as the Republican candidate challenging a Democratic state senator. However, surprisingly, Mr. Hyland still appointed Mr. Flanagan to the planning commission. Party affiliation was not important to Mr. Hyland. Mr. Hyland attended the town hall meeting to congratulate Mr. Flanagan on his retirement and to thank him for his service. The remarks that these two gentlemen shared on the podium moved everyone in the audience.

Mr. Hyland shared that he appointed Mr. Flanagan for the role because he was eminently qualified. He then added that he was convinced that Mr. Flanagan would have done a good job as the supervisor had he been elected in the election back in 1991 when they ran against each other. Mr. Flanagan responded that the reason why he challenged Mr. Hyland was not because Mr. Hyland had done a poor job as the supervisor, but rather because he simply wanted to do the supervisor's work. He praised Mr. Hyland for having been an excellent supervisor for so long.

While listening to the exchange of the compliments from the eighty-one-year-old retired supervisor and the ninety-three-year-old planning commissioner who would soon be retiring, I remembered proverbs like, "one word can pay off all your debts" and "praise can even make the whales dance." I should only speak kind words from now on.

Bill Gates

The Korea Times-Washington D.C.
March 16, 2011

I attended an evening meeting that was sponsored by the Economic Club in Washington D.C. last week. This club regularly invites celebrities to hear their stories, and the guest that day was none other than Bill Gates.

It was the first time that I had an opportunity to see Bill Gates in person as I had only encountered him through media until then. I was warned that it would not be much fun because he was not very sociable and not that good at public speaking, either; yet, just being able to see one of the most influential people in the world up close was enough to trigger all sorts of excitement.

This meeting was moderated by the chairman of the club, David Rubenstein. Coincidentally, on the way to that meeting, I heard the news on radio in the car that Mr. Rubenstein had donated ten million dollars to the Kennedy Center.[63] As the founder of the Carlyle Group, he is said to have donated about twenty-three million dollars to the Kennedy Center thus far.

As it is well known to everyone, Bill Gates is the co-founder of Microsoft and still serves as its Chairman. He used to be known as the richest person in the world for a long time, but he recently fell to the second place with a net worth of about fifty-six billion dollars.[64] However, he would still be undoubtedly the

---

63 One of the best-known performing arts center in the U.S., located in Washington, D.C.

64 According to the report published by the Forbes magazine on October 3, 2019, Bill Gates' individual wealth was estimated to be 106 billion dollars.

richest person, with the total wealth of about eighty-eight billion dollars if you combined all donations he has made to his charitable foundation, the Bill & Melinda Gates Foundation, founded with his wife in 2000.

The meeting with Bill Gates that evening took the form of a talk show with Chairman Rubenstein. I was impressed with the fact that Mr. Gates was a lot more talkative and had a better sense of humor than I had expected.

At Harvard where he attended college, all freshmen lived in dormitories located on the main campus called Harvard Yard. From sophomore year, the students would then move out to the dorms called a "House", reserved for upperclassmen. Instead of living in one of Harvard's traditional "River Houses" along the Charles River, Bill Gates volunteered to live in a dormitory beside the old Radcliffe College, a bit further off from the main Harvard campus. The reason, he cited, was a relatively lower ratio between female and male students. While the ratio in the River Houses was 3 to 1, it was about 1 to 1 where he chose. The River Houses were far more popular among men. He thought that he would have a better chance to meet and date female students by living in his dormitory. He confessed, however, that he was still not that successful. Everyone burst out laughing. He did not get married until 1994[65] when he was thirty-eight years old and was already a billionaire.

He stepped down from the day-to-day operations at the Microsoft in 2008 and now focuses mainly on the work of the foundation. He said that promoting global health and improving educational opportunities were the main projects of the Foundation. He believed that it would be impossible for people from poor third-world countries to get a proper education and develop their countries without having healthy bodies first. That was why his foundation took the lead in combating various

65 Bill Gates and his wife announced in May 2021 that they were ending their 27-year marriage, and the divorce was finalized in August 2021.

diseases and researching medicines. He also shared his deep interest in the reform of public education and emphasized the importance of improving the teacher evaluation system.

Bill Gates received an honorary doctorate from his alma mater Harvard years ago, but he never actually graduated from it. He dropped out in 1975, his junior year, to devote himself to working on Microsoft, which he founded in the same year. Not surprisingly, his father, an attorney, strongly opposed his decision to give up college. A question related to this was raised during the Q&A session held after the conversation, and his answer caught my heart.

He was asked what he would do if any of his three children wanted to give up school in the middle and wanted to do something else. Bill Gates first laughed at this question and said without hesitation that his case was an exception and that it was not recommendable for everyone to give up studies and to do other work in the middle. He would oppose even more strongly than his own father had done. I felt that Bill Gates was not much different from any other parent. He had the heart of a parent who would be concerned about their children straying from their normal course of life.

In addition, he said that the inheritance that his children would receive would be sufficient to support whatever they wanted to do in the future, but not enough to do nothing. From that comment, I could glimpse thoughtfulness of a parent who would not want his children to grow up living off their inheritance without putting in any of their own effort just because they had rich parents. The meeting with Bill Gates helped me realize that there were many things that I could learn from him as an individual and as a father.

Eugene James Coleman

The Korea Times–Washington D.C.
September 11, 2015

Eugene James Coleman graduated from Mount Vernon High School in Fairfax County three years ago. During his senior year, he was the student representative to the school board and attended the meetings on behalf of all students in the county's public schools. He was usually called as "EJ", the initials from his name Eugene James, and I have occasionally heard news about him even after he graduated.

EJ went on to the Military Academy at West Point and is currently in his senior year. I recently learned some good news about him that had just become his class's first captain as well as its class president at the same time. This was only the third time in the entire history of West Point for that to happen.

Class presidents are elected by their peers at the Academy, but the first captain is appointed by the Superintendent of the Academy. The first captain is recognized to be the top leader for the entire Academy of more than forty-five hundred cadets. It is rare for someone to hold the two positions at the same time because each position has great responsibilities. You must be extraordinary to assume both roles at the same time.

The only two other former cadets who had simultaneously held the two positions were General John Pershing, graduated in 1886, and Brigadier General Pete Dawkins, graduated in 1959. John Pershing became the General of the Armies—the highest possible rank, equivalent to a six-star general—in 1919 for the first time in the history of the U.S. Army after making remarkable contributions during the World War I. The only other soldier who had risen to the position of the General of the Armies other than

John Pershing was George Washington, the first President of the U.S.—the designation was given to him only in 1975, 179 years after his death.

Pete Dawkins did not rise to the high position like John Pershing as a soldier, but he was awarded the Heisman Trophy, the highest honor for college football players, during his time at the Academy. He also studied at the University of Oxford as a Rhodes Scholar. He became the youngest ever army general in 1981. After retiring from the army, he held senior executive positions at Lehman Brothers, Primerica, Bain & Company, Citigroup, and Travelers Insurance, among others.

I was so proud that EJ, now mentioned in the same breath as these other famous people, had come from Fairfax County. Moreover, he had also been a student representative to the school board, a feat not too many black students had achieved in Fairfax County. The recent honor at the Academy was also a first for an African American. I felt grateful for the opportunities that I had to discuss some educational policies with this history-making individual, even if just for one year, and to witness a part of his growth as a young man and a leader in person.

EJ grew up with parents who emphasized the importance of education even though they were not wealthy. His parents were creative in finding ways to provide educational opportunities during his childhood. They wrote vocabulary words on index cards and put them on many places around the house like doors, refrigerator, and tables, so that he could read and memorize the words. His parents allowed him to eat ice cream only after correctly identifying the color of the treat and spelling it out. They demonstrated that you did not have to particularly spend a lot of money to create learning opportunities. However, when it came to important decisions, he made them for himself. It was his decision to choose West Point as the only school he wanted to attend when applying for college.

EJ started learning to fly planes as a hobby at the age of thirteen and obtained a license a year later. As a member of the airborne forces while also actively working on boxing, bodybuilding, and even scuba diving, he will be on mandatory duty for the next five years once he graduates from West Point. What he will do after that is unpredictable at this point; however, many people who have watched him until now hope for him to remain in the military and become a general someday. According to his mother, he has a plan to run for an elected office before 2032, though I cannot speak to the significance of why it must be 2032 specifically. I felt that his mother was being selective with her words although she already knew what position he was planning to challenge. There are many fans who will enthusiastically support him whatever options he chooses, and of course, I am one of them. EJ, keep it up!

With Eugene James Coleman at his graduation celebration

Noah Kim And Grandfather

The Korea Times-Washington D.C.
December 8, 2017
December 7, 2018
Updated: March 10, 2020

Noah Kim was a football player at Westfield High School in Fairfax County. With a height of six foot three, he also played on the basketball team, but football was his better sport. He was the quarterback, in charge of the team's offense.

I often go to watch high school football games. It is not just because I am a school board member. The first couple of high school friends whom I befriended after coming to the U.S. had often taken me to high school football and basketball games. I had watched some basketball games even back in Korea, but football was totally unfamiliar to me. It was hard to follow where the ball was going, especially when the quarterback passed the ball to another player right after taking it from the center.

The high school that I graduated from in the U.S. was the same school appeared in the famous movie *Remember the Titans*. The movie was based the true story of what happened to my high school's football team when Alexandria City schools were integrated in the early 1970s. Denzel Washington played the lead role in the movie as the black coach of an integrated football team.

The first time I had met Noah was during his freshman year in high school. He was a backup player at the time, so I was not able to see him play until the following year when he became a sophomore. Not many sophomores start in games, meaning that Noah must have been a good player to start as a sophomore. A few years ago, the Westfield High School football team became Virginia state champions for the third consecutive year. The opposing team in all three state finals was Oscar Smith High School, located near the City of Norfolk in the southeastern part of Virginia. It is probably the only time in the history of Virginia high school football for the same two teams to meet in the finals for three consecutive years. The third time Westfield won the final was with Noah as a sophomore starting quarterback.

I mentioned Noah in my newspaper column a week before the third final. A few days later, I received a phone call from an elderly Korean man. He introduced himself as Noah's grandfather. He also told me the name of the Korean restaurant that he used to operate in the past. Once I heard the name, I knew exactly where the restaurant was and who the caller was—I used to go to eat in that restaurant.

Noah Kim with his grandfather at his ceremony to sign a letter of intent to go to Michigan State University and play football there

The elderly man and I exchanged some pleasantries and I congratulated him for having such a wonderfully gifted grandson. I also added that Noah was not only good at football but also very handsome. Then, the elderly man laughed as if he had been waiting for the word and exclaimed, "Ah, that's all because he has actually taken after me!" It was a happy admission from a proud grandfather.

After that day, I often went to watch football games of Noah's team. One game when Noah was a junior, Westfield had the ball with the score tied at 7–7 with 8 minutes left in the second quarter. Noah ran to the left with the ball, and it looked like he might have been running an option play.[66] A player from the opposing team chased closely after him. Noah looked for a player to whom he could pass the ball, but it did not look good. He should have thrown away the ball at that point, but he did not.

He was tackled by a group of five or six opposing players. Noah was buried at the bottom of the heap. The referee blew his whistle and the players stood up one by one, except Noah. The stadium suddenly fell silent, and everyone held their breath. The trainer ran out to the field and started examining Noah's entire body. Many players from both teams seemed to be praying, with some kneeling on knees and some covering their heads with their hands.

After a while, Noah began to move. The crowd and the players finally were able to breathe a sigh of relief. However, Noah was injured and was eventually put on a stretcher to be taken to an ambulance. Noah's father seemed to be trying to manage his expressions in witnessing the whole situation. Tears welled up in his white mother's eyes. The legendary thirty-seven-game winning streak of the Westfield High School football team ended that day.

Noah, with a broken femur, had to give up the winter basketball season that year and went into rehabilitation. Fortunately, he was able to fully recover and return to football before the start of the season in the following year. After Noah's

---

66 An option play in football refers to an offensive play designed for the quarterback to either pass, run, or hand the ball off to another player depending on the situation after it is given to him by the center.

return, the Westfield team went into a postseason after ending the regular season with a good record. However, regrettably, it lost to another team from Fairfax County, South County High School, in the semi-final match of the Virginia state championship. The South County team then played against Oscar Smith in the final and won the championship. Thus, Oscar Smith ended up losing four times in the finals to Fairfax County teams.

A few months later, I received a phone call from Noah's grandfather again. I was to be honored with an award at a football event that I attended every year. The award was given in recognition of my many years of support and interest for football while serving on the school board. Coincidentally, Noah was chosen as one of the Player of the Year award recipients at the same event. I was given a chance to give some remarks after receiving the award. I shared with the audience the phone conversation that I had with Noah's grandfather in the past. My intention was to congratulate Noah, as well as to urge him not to forget that his grandfather was proud of him.

My remark must have been then relayed to Noah's grandfather on the same evening, as he phoned me the next morning. He thanked me for the interest that I had shown in Noah over the years. He then told me that Noah's father used to be good at sports as well, but that he had to stay in the restaurant from 7 a.m. until midnight every day to run the business instead of being there when Noah's father needed some additional support from him. As such, he felt that he had not been able to provide the proper support for his son's athletic career. He expressed his regrets for the past and noted that it seemed that Noah was finally fulfilling a dream that his father could not achieve.

After high school, Noah will be entering Michigan State University in the fall on a football scholarship. I am not sure whether he will start as a freshman or will need to spend some time first warming bench. Either way, I hope that I might see him on TV in near future. He may even play for a professional team at some point. I wish him well in his long journey ahead.

With Noah Kim's family after a football game
Noah Kim's family on a hike

Jay Pearson

The Korea Times–Washington D.C.
August 22, 2014

I attended a summer high school graduation ceremony two weeks ago. This graduation ceremony was for students who had earned the required credits through summer school to graduate. Most of these students had experienced many ups and downs through their high school years, and so, the graduation ceremony had a more special meaning to them. There usually are at least a few of these students from almost every high school in Fairfax County each year.

The keynote speech was given by Mr. Jay Pearson this year. He used to be the principal at Marshall High School until just a couple of months ago. His speech, which I had previously heard at another graduation ceremony for special education students, was about his life's journey. I am writing his story here with his permission.

Mr. Pearson was recently promoted to become an executive principal with the reorganization of the central administrative office of Fairfax County Public Schools (FCPS).[67] Prior to the reorganization, FCPS used to be divided into eight clusters. Each cluster was assigned an assistant superintendent and a director who were responsible for directing and supervising approximately twenty-five schools. It is now reorganized into five regions with each region having one assistant superintendent and one or two executive principals to take charge of around forty schools.

Previously, the cluster directors supported their assistant

---

67 Mr. Jay Pearson was further promoted since then to become a regional assistant superintendent before retiring in June 2021. He graduated from the same T.C. Williams Senior High School several years after I had.

superintendents, but their positions used to be below the job levels of the principals. As such, it was not easy to find good applicants for the director positions among principals, and there was some confusion about the command structure. For that reason, the new positions of executive principals were created, and they are now above the job levels of the principals. They are also considered to be strategically placed with good opportunities and prospects for promotion to assistant superintendent positions.

Mr. Pearson had been a principal for nine years and is an excellent educator. He was named the "Principal of the Year" in FCPS last year. He shared that he did not necessarily do well while in school himself, and not everything had gone smoothly for him. Sure, he had received some As, but there were also many Bs and Cs. He planned to go to Middlebury College in Vermont to major in French or University of Virginia to study computer science after high school. He did not know why he was thinking about French and computer science when they were not particularly connected with each other. Furthermore, to become a computer science major, he had to be good in mathematics, but he was not—he had almost failed Algebra 2.[68] In fact, he did not even apply for college in his high school senior year. No, that did not mean that he had already secured a job to work after graduation, either. He did eventually get a job as a shuttle bus driver for a rental car company at an airport after graduation.

At first, working as a shuttle bus driver and having conversations with new passengers every day were fun. He earned some money and bought a new car. He also left his parents' house to become independent from his parents.

But when he looked at himself after a year, he realized that he could not continue to live his life like that, so he registered for a two-year program at Northern Virginia Community College as a start. He then transferred to George Mason University a year later

68 At the time, Algebra 2 was the level of math where quadratic equations were introduced.

and began working on his major in international studies, as he had now wanted to become a diplomat. He also moved back into his parents' house to save on expenses and continued working part-time while studying. He finally earned his bachelor's degree after four years.

However, he was unable to become a diplomat and did not find a stable job right away. By chance, he got a job as a temporary substitute teacher, and that opened his eyes to the teaching profession. He later became a fulltime history teacher at a high school. Since then, he has gradually risen to his current position over twenty-four years by teaching diligently and caring for students and other educators along the way. He attributed his hard work and search for his most suitable path without giving up as the main factors behind his success, even though his start was not that smooth.

We can easily find around us the students who may not be doing well in school. There are also quite a few young people who have difficulties in finding a job after graduating. To them, I would like to share Mr. Pearson's stories and ask them not to give up the hope but to try harder.

Jay Pearson is in the middle. The one on the left is Maribeth Luftglass, who retired in June 2020 from her position as Chief Technology Officer of the Fairfax County Public Schools.

George Towery

The Korea Times-Washington D.C.
September 8, 2017

There was an educator who retired in 2010 after serving forty years as an elementary school principal in Fairfax County. The first ten years were at Lorton Elementary School and the next thirty years at Cameron Elementary School.

Cameron Elementary School has a high percentage of at-risk students. When he was first appointed there as the principal, around sixty percent of the students were from families in poverty and around seventy percent from families where English was not their first language. Even now, around two-thirds of the students are from poor families and around a half receive the ESOL services. However, this principal had continued to work for thirty years in that school until his retirement despite all the challenges the high percentage of at-risk student population had presented. He had declined opportunities to move to other schools more than a few times over the years.

This school had also been famous for its programs for students considered to be problematic. Trust has been built among the school board members that this school could provide a more effective education for students with problematic classroom attitudes or behaviors. At the center of this such trust were Mr. Towery's personality, dedication, and educational philosophy.

Sadly, he passed away last month—he was only seventy-three years old, still quite young. I attended a gathering held to commemorate his death and to honor his life. The gathering was filled with fellow educators, his former students, parents, and friends. Mr. Towery's pictures and some artifacts were displayed.

While I was looking closely at the displays, something caught my attention—a report card from his high school chemistry class. I could not close my mouth the moment I saw the grades. The final year-end grade was a C; however, the end of marking periods grades included Ds and Fs. Both final exam grades were Fs. Certainly not something to brag about, but there must have been a reason for displaying the report card. It could not have been to inform people why he did not major in chemistry. I imagine that, instead, it was perhaps to share a message that you could still become a well-respected educator even if you had poor grades in some subjects while in school. Parents should also not expect their children to excel in all subjects.

Mr. Towery has an unusual record of becoming a principal at the young age of twenty-seven, after only five years in education. He had worked four years as a teacher before becoming an assistant principal. Only a year later was he then appointed as a principal. Such rapid succession of promotions was clear proof of his exceptional ability as an educator. He was honored with a "Principal of the Year" award, the first time for an elementary school principal in Fairfax County to receive such award.

He compiled his experiences in a book published in 2012. The title is Touched by a Child and is easy reading. The book includes the following stories:

-Alfredo, a very handsome five-year old student, who liked to kick other students and the adults. When asked for the reason, he replied that his father beat his mother whenever he got angry.

-Alex, another handsome five-year old student, was abandoned at the door of someone else's house right after he was born. He lived with his adoptive parents until he found his birth father when he turned five. His father suddenly became a single father. The father had to work at night, so Alex had no choice but to stay with the babysitter at night.

-Thomas, with hearing and speech impairments, expressed his frustration with violent behaviors.

-Ronald was only in the fifth grade, but he already had a long history of drug use.

His stories show that there are many students around us who suffer with serious life challenges. Mr. Towery stresses the point that there are also many educators who teach these students without giving up on them. He also tells us that these students, like everyone else, have the right to live their lives fully and that it is incumbent on all of us to help them do just that. Mr. Towery left us after showing that he himself had lived according to his own teaching.

| *Postscript* |

As noted in the Preface, this book is an English version of my book titled Sky Castle School Board Member Stories, published in Korean last year. As a Korean-American attorney, I translate legal documents from Korean to English and vice versa from time to time. However, I had never translated a whole book and did not appreciate how difficult this task would prove to be. My brain has been tested to its maximum capability in finding the most suitable English counterparts for many nuanced Korean words and expressions. Not only are there differences in sentence structures and grammar, but the sociocultural differences behind the words used have also presented challenges.

With nine months of that effort now over, I will rest a little. Yet, with more than six hundred previously published newspaper columns still left in reserve, I know that I will want to publish a couple more books. The second book will focus on intimate and warm stories, followed by a third book to include some deeper stories, even stories I have not yet had the courage to share publicly. By the time I get to work on this book, I hope that I will have grown a little more mature to openly sharing these stories.

The King James Bible Dictionary defines a "sojourner" as "a temporary resident; a stranger or traveler who dwells in a place for a time." The first time I gave much thought to this word was when I was doing research about thirty years ago on the history of American immigration. Many of the early European immigrants thought of themselves as "sojourners". They came to the U.S. to earn money but not necessarily to stay. They wanted to return to their home countries once they earned enough money to support their families and to pursue their dreams back home. However, most of them eventually ended up staying in the U.S. Even before I wondered why that had been the case, I realized that I was not in any way different from them.

When my father first mentioned the idea about immigrating to the U.S., I resented it. Why would I desert my home country to go live in a foreign land with completely different culture? I told him that I did not want to go, even though I knew that I had no choice. Even while I was studying at Harvard, I wanted to find a way to return to Korea once I completed my education in the U.S. That pursuit began changing during my law school years, and I finally acquired my American citizenship in 1983, about nine years after I had first arrived in the U.S.

Looking back at more than forty-seven years of my immigrant journey in the U.S., I must admit that I have been blessed with many things. No worries about ever not having enough food to eat or not being able to afford high school tuition. Sufficient financial aid and loans to attend college and law school; being able to do honest work to earn honest income to support my family; and, yes, two wonderful American-born sons who are pursuing their own American dreams. Of course, I have also had the opportunity to provide public service for twenty-five years. I am grateful. In as much as I still terribly miss what I left behind back in Korea, I know where I want to live.

That does not mean that my journey in the U.S. has been always smooth. Not so, not so. Starting with the language, I had to learn everything anew and adapt to the new surroundings. I am, in fact, still learning and adapting. I will never be able to learn and adapt enough to feel completely comfortable living in the U.S., but that is all right. That makes life more fun. I need to stay alert and that is a challenge I am willing to take.

| Index |

A

B

C

D

E

F

G

H

I

J

K

M

N

U

V

W

스카이캐슬 교육위원 이야기

2020 I ₩15,000 I 296 pages

The above is the Korean version of this book. The Korean version books may be purchased in bookstores in Korea or by contacting the author at **skycastlemoon@gmail.com** in the U.S.